Anxi

Mindfulness for Beginners

&

Holistic Relaxation

By Marta Tuchowska

Copyright © 2016 by Marta Tuchowska

Free complimentary audiobook available at:

www.holisticwellnessproject.com/mindfulness

All rights reserved. No part of this publication may be reproduced, stored in a retrieval system, or transmitted, in any form or by any means, electronic, mechanical, photocopying, recording or otherwise, without the prior written permission of the author and the publishers.

All information in this book has been carefully researched and checked for factual accuracy. However, the author and publishers make no warranty, expressed or implied, that the information contained herein is appropriate for every individual, situation or purpose, and assume no responsibility for errors or omission. The reader assumes the risk and full responsibility for all actions, and the author will not be held liable for any loss or damage, whether consequential, incidental, special or otherwise that may result from the information presented in this publication. By purchasing this book you have agreed to the aforementioned statement.

Contents

Book 1 7
Mindfulness for Beginners..7
Introduction 9
Chapter 1 What Mindfulness Is Not 11
   Simple Rules of Mindfulness 11
   Mindfulness & Awareness 13
Chapter 2 Transforming Your Life with Mindfulness 14
   Mindfulness & Relationships 14
   Mindfulness and Honesty..15
   Awareness. Real awareness. Knowing ourselves. 15
   What Kills Mindfulness? 17
Chapter 3 Mindfulness to Make Friends with Your Emotions and Enjoy Your Life Now 19
   Be Hungry for Mindfulness 20
   How to Actually Practice Mindfulness? 20
   Mindfulness Exercises 24
   Inner Mindfulness - How to Make GOOD Friends with Your Emotions 27
Chapter 4 Transform All Areas of Your Life and Health with Mindful Self-Honesty 30
   Breathe out mindless illusions... 31
   Practicing Mindfulness in Everyday Situations 33
   Mindfulness and Honest Self-Love...35
   Mindfulness for Ordinary People 38
   Is ego always bad?...39

Chapter 5 Mindfulness for Deep Transformation and Long-Lasting Change 41

Mindfulness and Overprotecting Others 41

Mindfulness and Journaling 42

What I really mindfully want 43

What mindful actions will I take? 43

What will I mindfully give up? 44

Mindfulness and Criticizing Others 45

Mindfulness for Anxiety 46

Mindfulness for Laziness 46

Mindfulness and Shiny Object Syndrome 48

Mindfulness to Let Go and Achieve Peace 48

Mindfulness and Gratitude 49

Conclusion 51

Book 2 52

Holistic Relaxation- Erase Anxiety! 52

Effective Natural Therapies, Stress Management Techniques, Holistic Remedies, and Wellness Coaching for Busy People 52

Introduction 54

Disclaimer 66

Chapter 1 Stress- a Blessing in Disguise? 68

Environmental factors 69

Use and abuse of various substances 70

Medical factors 70

Genetics 71

Chapter 2 Body and Mind Techniques for Holistic Relaxation 74

Progressive relaxation 74

Autogenic training 77

Applied relaxation 79
Meditation 80
Stress-free wellness zone! 82
MEDITATION 85
FIVE SENSES DEEP MEDITATION TECHNIQUE 85
Chapter 3 Phytotherapy for Stress Management 89
St John's Wort (Hypericum perforatum) 90
Passion flower (Passiflora) 93
Valerian (Valeriana Officinalis) 95
Hawthorn Berry (Crateagus Oxycanthus) 97
MORE NATURAL HERBAL SOLUTIONS 99
Chapter 4 Homeopathy and Bach Flower Remedies 107
Bach Flower Remedies 116
Chapter 5 Yoga for Holistic Relaxation 121
Yoga 123
Sukhasana (Easy Pose) 124
Matsyasana (The Fish Pose) 124
Setubandhasana (The Bridge Pose) 125
Shirshasana (The Headstand) 125
Marjariasana (The Cat Stretch) 126
Adhomukha Shwanasana (The Downward-Facing Dog) 126
Paschimottanasana (Seated Forward Bend) 127
Vrkshasana (Tree Pose) 128
Halasana (Plough Pose) 128
Relax with Tai-Chi 131
Chapter 6 Holistic Nutrition 135
Chapter 7 Mind over Matter 146

Chapter 8: Aromatherapy and Massage 150
Bonus Chapter: Learn Holistic Facial Massage 154
    Holistic Facial Massage Tutorial 156
Conclusion 160

Book 1

Mindfulness for Beginners

How to Drastically Transform All Areas of Your Life & Health with Powerful Mindfulness Techniques (That Anyone Can Master)

By Marta Tuchowska

Copyright © 2016 by Marta Tuchowska

Introduction

Let me start with a bold statement - if you are a seeker type of person, you have probably read different self-help, personal development, and spirituality books and still feel like you have a lot of self-improvement work to do. Maybe you feel stuck or overwhelmed with all of the information you've gathered. The book you are reading now aims to make your journey simple, doable, and fun.

It's a fluff-free, practical guide designed to help you make friends with mindfulness and make it your lifestyle so that you can get honest with yourself and enjoy the process of your transformation. There will be no rainbows or unicorns because the approach I want to take is to understand and accept our reality first so that we know where we are. As soon as we know where we are, we can take the necessary action to change our direction if needed.

So while I can't promise the world, and I am definitely not a spiritual guru and do not want to become one, I am really excited for this mindfulness journey we are just about to embark on together. As always, I write in a simple, conversational style. I want you to feel as if you are talking to a friend over a nice cup of coffee. In this case- a mindfulness cup of coffee that will help you awaken your mind and soul to help you take necessary actions aligned with your true self. This is how you will be able to start transforming your life the way you want. Through the following pages of this book, you will first learn what mindfulness really is and how it translates to awareness, self-love, and self-honesty. You will then learn how to apply mindfulness in different life situations so that you can enjoy better quality of life.

Sound good?

Without further ado, let's get down to it!

****

I have a free complimentary audiobook (+ free newsletter) for you. Visit:

www.HolisticWellnessProject.com/mindfulness

to secure your free copy now!

Chapter 1 What Mindfulness Is Not

There are many books on mindfulness and many definitions of what mindfulness is, what it's not, and how you can achieve this mindful lifestyle quickly in certain amount of steps if you attend the guru's X seminar or buy his expensive certification program. Don't get me wrong, I have nothing against retreats or programs. There is always something to learn. However, the approach I take on in this book is a really simple, common sense approach. The definitions and explanations I present are based on my own experiences with mindfulness and how I use it to improve my health, life, career, and relationships, and how you can use it too. This book is not about me, it's about you.

Simple Rules of Mindfulness

Here's what I believe mindfulness is all about:

-It's a state that helps you notice things as they are - not too negative and not too positive. You see and realize things exactly as they are, without any judgment or unnecessary emotions that can result in anxious states.

-Mindfulness helps us be more aware. Awareness takes some time to master, and even the most spiritual gurus never master it fully. When we are aware, we can dive deep and learn how to solve our problems in a holistic way. Now, when I say holistic, I'm not referring to herbs, homeopathy, or essential oils (don't get me wrong, I am really into all this stuff, but there is much more to the word "holistic"). By saying "holistic", I mean taking a "whole-istic" approach and getting to the root of the problem. This may mean getting a bit uncomfortable and asking yourself questions that make you leave your comfort zone. For example, a person may tend to overspend or have a few too many drinks here and there. It may take some time to dive deep and understand the root of the problem - maybe this person is trying to escape sadness and loneliness? Maybe they need instant relaxation, which is what shopping and drinking provides to them? By becoming more aware of the situation, they can actually take action to do something about it. Mind that I have nothing against shopping, buying nice things, or enjoying an occasional drink with a good friend. It's when we are not aware of what we are really doing that our habits may turn problematic. So this is where mindfulness can help develop self-awareness

-Mindfulness is like a muscle. If you feel like you are not mindful, it's simply because you need to spend more time growing and stretching this muscle. This is something that many people overlook, and I have been guilty of this as well. After all, there are so many things to focus on in this day and age! We want to be happier, slimmer, more successful and what not. But... the good news is that when we try to practice mindfulness, achieving success, health, and whatever it is we have on our goal list becomes a lot easier. Yes, I know it all sounds a bit hippie dippie combined with an over marketed line, "Just be mindful and love yourself, and you will achieve health, wealth, and happiness in 7 days or less. Click here to learn how, for only $697. Can be paid in 7 easy installments!"

We get exposed to lines like, "Raise your awareness, raise your consciousness, even raise your pH and it will all be fine." But really, it takes some work, commitment, and honest moments of realization of what you actually can or can't do. My goal for this book is to show you how you can practice mindfulness in the real world as an ordinary person without overwhelming yourself with too many rituals or actions. The best thing about mindfulness? It's free. It always has been and always will be.

Mindfulness & Awareness

To me, mindfulness and awareness are really important topics, and you may find certain parts of this book a bit repetitive. I hope you will forgive me. You see, I really want to make sure that I communicate well so that you understand my point well.

So how can mindfulness help you take your life to a whole new level? That phrase also sounds a bit over market-ish now that I think about it...

To make it simple - the more we practice mindfulness, the more aware we become. This is how we can make better decisions aimed at achieving a better life. We make better and healthier choices. Personally, I have noticed a massive improvement in my health and fitness thanks to mindfulness. Why? Because I was able to analyze negative patterns and habits. With mindfulness, I was able to embrace healthy mindful eating and healing. I found it very helpful to eradicate my emotional eating patterns. We will talk more about that later in this book.

Also, mindfulness helps us focus on where we're going, not where we're coming from. By taking a mindful approach, we learn from our mistakes. It's not about denying that bad things happened. Unfortunately, in this world, bad things can happen even to the most positive people. There is no guarantee for an eternally stress-free and problem-free life. But...mindfulness gives us tools to be proactive, not reactive.

Chapter 2 Transforming Your Life with Mindfulness

Mindfulness can also help you excel in your career. It helps you to dive deep to learn your strengths, what you're good at, and what you're not so good at. You will know what to focus on.

Mindfulness can even help you to gradually define your passions. For most people, including myself, it takes some time to get to know your passions, so don't worry if you are still trying to figure out what you're passionate about. You're not alone.

Besides, your passions and interests may always change. Mindfulness helps you become more aware of those shifts so that you can adapt and, if possible, change or re-adjust your professional path.

The same applies to relationships!

Mindfulness & Relationships

From my experience, most problems that people face in their relationships come from the following mistakes (and we have all been guilty of them):

-Not being able to communicate well.

-Not knowing what we really want.

-Expecting people to be perfect even though we are not.

-Not listening to other people, but demanding that they listen to us.

-Having either too much ego, or being too ashamed of oneself (both can be detrimental, I believe some levels of ego can be helpful for a healthy personal development, more on that later).

Mindfulness and Honesty

Honesty is lesson number 1. Before we really get into it, we must accept this Universal truth and become more humble. The truth is that we are asleep and the level of our mindfulness and awareness are low.

Even if we have been through programs on mindfulness, attended courses, and read books, we are still asleep, or almost asleep, and we still don't know it all. We might know enough to get started on living and practicing our mindful lifestyles, but again, we must accept the fact that we don't know it all and we will never know it all. There is no certification that will make us know it all or seem that we know it all.

This may be a hard pill to swallow, but I consider it to be a very important mantra. This mantra will teach us to be humble so that we can remain hungry. Hungry for what?

Awareness. Real awareness. Knowing ourselves.

Be hungry for awareness, put your ego down, and use this statement as a starting point.

Ego is a good thing in a mindful world. I believe that ego is great if it translates into passion, ambition, drive, and providing value to other people.

Ego can be detrimental if it makes us stop our quest by making us think that we know it all and there is nobody we can learn from. This can be very misleading for all of us, hence the mantra I mentioned earlier. This mantra will help us stay on the ground.

The truth is that our mind is always wandering. We can't stop what's on our mind, we can't have it blank. But we can be aware of what is going on and read through it to learn more about ourselves.

So this is good news if you have ever tried to meditate...

Maybe you got frustrated with meditation because you were not able to quieten your mind as much as you aimed for. No worries, you are not alone.

It's not possible to quieten your mind 100%, just like it's not possible to be 100% self-conscious. I think it is good news in a way. Nobody is perfect!

Also, remembering what was on our mind or what we saw does not always mean being self-conscious. We can remember all the details but still miss on the big picture.

Finally, we need to accept hard work, yes hard work, through mindfulness. It's like lifting some heavy weights to tone up your mindfulness muscles.

Reading this book alone will not help you become more mindful. You will need to take action and start practicing the techniques that I will show you and promise yourself you will not feel scared of self-honesty and diving deep.

You will do yourself a favor and look at yourself, your life, your actions, and thoughts from the outside. You will admit to yourself both the good and bad, exactly like it is. During this process, you may start feeling uncomfortable. There might be some shifts on your way. I am not saying this to be negative, I am saying this to help you prepare yourself for this journey.

The prize will be unleashing the power of mindfulness and awareness.

No shortcuts are needed. People often resort to drugs to achieve states of awareness, but instead of getting closer to those states, they are just getting further away from them.

Instead of getting rid of layers that prevent us from achieving a life full of happiness, drugs and other toxic substances only add to those layers and distractions.

What Kills Mindfulness?

There are also other things that kill mindfulness:

- Distractions - I'm referring to all kinds of addictions, even social media, shopaholism, and even some kinds of workaholism (I have been guilty of a few of those).

- Judgment - Here I'm referring to both positive and negative judgment. For example, some people are a bit naïve and believe in everything they see and hear. It's easy to manipulate them. These people will be the first ones to get manipulated by all kinds of advertisements and are very easy to be sold to. On the other hand, there are also people who are too negative, and they see dishonesty in all human beings. Both approaches lack mindfulness and what I call real personal investigation. They also very often reflect the relationships that people have had with themselves and what has happened to them in the past.

I would be dishonest to say I have never judged. Another mantra by Marta is: *We have all judged and we have all been judged, it's just how the world goes.*

I also believe that as long as we are alive, we will judge and be judged to some extent.

However, mindfulness can help us reduce the amount of judgment that very often results in suffering and unhappiness that we either get ourselves or create for other people.

Chapter 3 Mindfulness to Make Friends with Your Emotions and Enjoy Your Life Now

Mindless can mean "all the same." This can work out for some people, especially less sensitive people who feel good following the crowd. But if you are like me, and you have always felt a bit weird compared to your peers (I've had this feeling since I was a kid) and it means that you need to follow your own way. This is not to say that you and I are better than others. It's not about who is better or worse. It's about who decides to follow their truth of self-awareness. It's about who wants to feel re-awakened.

I know some people who are happy exactly where they are, doing what they are doing. I don't preach anything to them because I see them happy. Of course, if I were to live the way they live, I would not be happy, and I guess they would not be happy living their lives following my lifestyle. But again, it's not about who's right or wrong. It's about knowing yourself. Some people like to be asleep. Besides, all is subjective. I may think they are asleep, but they think they live their lives to the fullest. Again, who am I to judge those people?

Follow this definition - Mindful can mean different and unique. So don't worry if you have always had a feeling you were different. It's just the way you were meant to be. Maybe you have went through some pain, suffering, and rejection.

Maybe you cried thinking, "Why me? "Guess what, mindfulness can help you shift your perception. You can see your bad days, your pain, and your suffering as something that will provide inspiration to other people.

Be Hungry for Mindfulness

Every day, ask yourself for patience. This is what we all need. Patience is something that helps us enjoy our mindfulness cup of coffee even more!

Be grateful for who you are and accept yourself, but always look for that next level.

Mindfulness helps us embrace self-love, honest self-love, where there are also bad days. This is normal; we are not robots. We need those days to have a good and honest relationship with ourselves.

It's just like with a partner - you need to communicate well with each other. Now, think of yourself as your partner. Yes! Some people may judge you as egocentric, narcissistic, and who knows what else. Don't care about what others say.

For the time being, you only need to care about your mindfulness journey.

Put yourself first and take care of yourself so that you can transform yourself and take better care of those you love.

How to Actually Practice Mindfulness?

Even though you may not realize it, if you are reading this book carefully, just focusing on the current content and not getting too distracted thinking, "Why is this book so different compared to typical books on mindfulness?" You are already mindful.

Well, even if you do have such thoughts, this is absolutely normal. Perfection does not exist.

A spiritual guru would say that by being more mindful, we are less prone to judge, which is true. But a spiritual guru could also say that when we are mindless, we are quicker to judge, which is also true. However, by saying that, he is also kind of judging, right?

The way I see it is-just do the best you can, and whenever you get off track, get mindless and judgmental, and be aware of it. In other words, try to be mindful of your mindlessness, and try to be mindful of your dark side too.

In this day and age, we are very impatient. When it comes to books and information products... I recently invested in an online course related to marketing and entrepreneurship. To be honest, while going through the first lessons, I was thinking of returning it. I thought, "Man, this is just so basic!" Then I noticed that many people online were talking negatively about this course. I was actually disappointed in myself for buying it, and I was really on the verge of asking for refund. But then I wondered, how can I judge the course just by a few lessons? Why don't I give it a try and at least try to learn the rest of the material? Why do I trust other people's opinions? I haven't even studied all the lessons, and I have not applied them.

I therefore decided to re-watch the very first introductory lesson. While going through the course for the first time, I had skipped it, thinking that my time was too valuable to be wasted on the introduction. In this introduction, the creator of the course said just one thing. "Don't judge this course until you have watched all the lessons carefully." I decided to be mindful and had faith in the process. I realized that I was too biased and judgmental in my opinions. Subsequently, I watched the whole course and it gave me many brilliant ideas and strategies that I can now apply not only in my business, but to my life.

Other people missed it because they judged it just by the very few lessons they watched, and since it was different from the mainstream courses of this kind, they judged it too quickly. They were looking for this secret sauce that would make them successful. Then, instead of using their time carefully, they wasted it by going online and writing negative opinions about the course, even though they only did about 5 or 10% of it. They chose their own egos ("But I already know this stuff"!) and decided to stick to the same old, same old.

Of course, this is not about forcing yourself to like something you don't like or something that is not for you. Being mindful is not always super positive. It's about opening yourself up to learning and experience. It's about putting your ego down and being curious, like a kid.

Mindfulness will make you stronger so that you don't give up too early. And if you do give up, at least you will know that you tried your best.

I know people who come to yoga and they just give up after the very first lesson. They say: but I am not that flexible!

Can you see the *mindless pattern* here?

The best part is that they had already invested in fancy yoga mats and yoga pants only to say it was not for them!

Why? Most people are not mindful enough to realize that there is also a process and learning curve to everything. There is no reason to compare yourself to other people. For example, I could quit writing this book and say that I am not a good enough writer and English is my second language, or that I don't have the time to do it. And honestly, that is what the old Marta would say. However, the new Marta is more mindful now, and she knows the right dose of self-love and self-honesty. She knows how to trust her process and be mindful about it. Instead of focusing on problems, I focus on solutions. My super editor will heal this manuscript when needed and I am sure he will also have a few laughs at my English here and there!

Whatever it is that you need to do, there is always a learning curve. Even if you do something you are absolutely passionate about, there will always be certain mundane tasks that you will just have to do. This happens to me all the time. Again, mindfulness comes in very handy for me, both in my personal and professional life. Finally, thanks to mindfulness, you learn to be passionate about the process of whatever it is that you do.

I hope you got the general grasp of what mindfulness is and how it can be used in your everyday life. You can start being mindful right now. Don't give up thinking you are easily distracted or that it's not for you. By embracing mindfulness, you will have more quality of life and health, and you will be more successful in your career without overworking or overwhelming yourself.

The work I want you to do for the time being is very simple. Don't deviate from what I teach and do it every day. The simplicity of these exercises will make it easier for you to practice them every day, even when on holiday, and even when you're tired. Just give it a go! You can set up a daily alert on your mobile device to make sure you actually do these exercises.

Go for it and do them!

Mindfulness Exercises

The goal - Learn to perceive everything the way it is, both the good and the bad.

This is how you can be mindfully proactive and look for solutions.

Have the raw data of what's going on. By saying raw, I mean not through the lenses of your own emotions and meanings.

We will practice mindfulness through our senses and internal dialogues.

1. Sense: SEE

    Sit down, take a few deep breaths, and have a look at an object around you, preferably something static, like a table or cup. Look at it. Just notice it, that's it.
    I am looking at my cup of green tea now. I embrace its yellow color. I keep breathing and looking at the cup. I really enjoy just staring at it.

    By the way, if you are practicing this in an office or a room with other people, they will think you are going mad. I suggest you do it when you're on your own so that you can tune in better.

    Keep focusing on the object. Notice all of the colors and patterns. Just keep seeing and don't judge. We don't care where the object is coming from, we don't care whether we like it or not. It's just there and we are observing it.

    Good job, now it's time for the next step - our internal dialogue.

Register the fact that you are staring at the object. That's the only thing you are doing.

Again, focus on eliminating your opinions. Just focus on the facts that your eyes are registering. Close your eyes and focus on the image again. In my case, it's a big yellow cup with grey elements, filled with green tea. I just try to focus on the colors and shape, not on what I should do with the cup or where's it coming from.

It is the way it is and that's the way I register it.

Remember, this mindfulness exercise is just about savoring, and just about enjoying.

2. Hearing

Focus on what you can hear around you. Take a few deep breaths and focus.

In this day and age, we very often hear, but we don't truly listen. We are not mindful and not tuned in enough.

For now, just for a few minutes, all we need to do is to focus on what we can hear.

In my case, it is birds singing, some cars passing by, and my own breath. I don't give it any meaning.

What about you. What can you hear?

Now focus on your internal dialogue. Label it as it is. Note it as it is within reality.

3. Feeling

You can do this exercise either standing up or sitting down. It's up to you. Since I have been at my desk for quite a few hours now, I will stand up just to wake up a bit.

If standing up, all you need to do is stand up and be comfortable. Focus on the sensation between your feet and the floor.

If sitting down, all you need to do is to feel your butt (I know it sounds weird) or your feet touching the ground.

Now go inside and label it as it is. Without overcomplicating it. It doesn't matter how you judge it. Just focus on the essence. The raw essence. No cooking and no seasoning. Notice it the way it is. Keep breathing and noticing.

******

I hope you enjoyed this simple exercise. However, the best part is yet to come!

Unfortunately, this part is the most difficult and challenging for most of us. Luckily, this is what can result in optimal change that can shift us in the right direction - the direction we need to be in!

You see, in the previous exercise, we focused on outer sensations. But now it's time to dive deep and focus on inner sensations. This is what it's really all about, and this is where most people quit. Of course, I don't want you to quit, so bear with me. And even if you quit, don't judge yourself and the fact that you quit, because you can always re-commit and go back to it later. I quit many things many times in the past, but thanks to mindfulness, I was able to re-evaluate why I quit, and in many cases I decided to get back to certain activities and goals feeling stronger and more empowered.

OK, so let's do it! Have no fear!

Inner Mindfulness - How to Make GOOD Friends with Your Emotions

First of all, emotions are feedback. Yes, both good and bad emotions are feedback.

There is no reason for blocking out emotions and pretending it's OK. In this day and age of over-political correctness, where we all should appear as happy, proper, and just perfect, many of us tend to block our emotions.

I think this is a problem. I used to do it myself until one morning back in 2012. That morning, I just couldn't get out of bed. At that time, I was "OK," or I thought I was. I had a corporate job and was living for the weekends. Of course, there is nothing wrong with having a job if you enjoy it, or at least it does not affect your health in a negative way. So yeah, I thought I was OK, and I kept telling myself that it was OK because I was doing what everyone else around me was doing. Until one morning I just suddenly felt paralyzed. I thought, "What's happening, how is this possible? I am supposed to be a positive person. It's OK, I will be OK." But it wasn't OK. So I had to two choices: go and see a doctor and ask for some magic pills to be OK, or mindfully embrace the fact that it wasn't OK. Many of my friends back home thought that my life in a big city, abroad, in a sunny country was the ultimate dream, and so was a corporate job in multilingual customer service, obviously it was not for me. I was working myself towards sickness and exhaustion and I felt lost. At that time, I decided to be honest with myself. The first step was to honestly label how I felt without judging or correcting it.

And I knew I felt unfulfilled, emotionally drained, and disappointed with myself.

I realized I wasn't achieving my goals, but someone else's goals.

At that time, I could have gone on sick leave like many of my colleagues were doing, but I knew it would make things worse. So I just called my boss and apologized. I said that I overslept and I turned up to work a bit late, but man! I was changed.

At least I knew that what I was doing as far as my job was concerned was temporary. At least I knew I had to embrace self-care, mindfulness, and holistic personal development.

Some would say – oh, just quit your job! And yes, in many cases I agree. I evolved from an employee to an entrepreneur. However, we also need to be mindful about it. Most people can't afford to quit their jobs from one day to another, and usually it's not very smart or well thought out. I had done it before as well, only to end up looking for another job 2 or 3 months later.

This is why by embracing self-honesty, self-truth, and mindfulness, my mantra was, "This is not what I want to do for the rest of my life. But I am grateful for this position for the time being because it pays my bills and it will help me transition to a better career."

Now, this journey is a topic for another book and not really relevant now.

But mindfulness was my biggest remedy at that time.

I began researching and learning about meditation. At that time, as a fast-paced city girl, I thought meditation was a bit pointless, so it was a massive shift for me. Most guided meditations would not work for me, so I decided to create my own, simple one…

Marta's Mindfulness Meditation. I would just sit down and focus on all my senses. Sometimes with no logical order, just letting it go. Then I would do my inner mindfulness meditation and my inner scan, asking myself about how I felt. Then I would also journal without hiding anything from myself.

To sum up:

- Emotions are feedback. View them as colors, feel them as sensations, they just are.

Don't just hear them, actually *listen* to them. They are trying to guide you in a mindful way.

- All changes on your journey to mindfulness are a process. While retreats and seminars are great, you won't achieve your ultimate mindfulness mastery by paying a guru X for his latest product or workshop. You will need to do your own part and dive deep.

- It's absolutely normal to have weaker periods of time where you just feel a bit more negative, irritable or sad. Even the most positive people have those periods of time. While I am not a professional therapist or counselor, and I am not offering any specific advice for depressive or anxious states, I can only share my experience and the process that works for me. I simply slow down, tune in, and spend more time in meditation. I also try to be honest with myself and ask myself what I can do to move forward with the flow and how to make changes in my life in a mindful way.

- We can't always control what happens to us, but we can choose to be mindful about it. However, mindful will not always mean "but I am OK" even if you are not OK. Mindful means 'as it is now,' so don't be scared of giving yourself honest answers that will allow you make mindful decisions so that you can achieve real peace and happiness.

Chapter 4 Transform All Areas of Your Life and Health with Mindful Self-Honesty

Many of my subscribers reply to my newsletters saying that they either feel a deep sense of relief or sometimes they are just slightly surprised with my simple approach to mindfulness and life. While some, of course, may find my honesty and directness too overwhelming for them or are just not ready for it yet, many state that just by realizing that sometimes it's OK *not* to be OK, they realized that they no longer had to waste their energy masking the problem, but can actually use it to mindfully explore it.

In my *Holistic Mindfulness Newsletters,* I share the good and the bad about my journey. I have also noticed that many people get slightly surprised that I don't just write things like, "Hey, life is good, and it's always so beautiful and amazing because we are all mindful." I think that if someone has a bad day or there is something unpleasant going on in their lives, they may actually get pissed off when they receive a fluffy, over-feel good stuff like that. But I actually give simple strategies like in this book and underline one fact: *negative emotions are just feedback.*

Let me give you this example; it's the only one that comes to my mind now. Now, I am not a mom, so I am not giving any advice on parenting. It's just an example to illustrate my point:

Imagine a mom or dad with a small kid. The kid is crying, screaming, and pointing to their belly. What would most parents do? Well, most parents, assuming they are in their right senses, would assume that their kid is sick, probably suffering from food poisoning or maybe a bacteria, and would act quickly by taking their child to a doctor to see what the problem was and find a cure.

They would not just say to the kid, "Just smile, you are OK. Your belly is fine. Just be happy, and it will be fine. Just love yourself. Breathe in and out. You should be fine now!"

I hope you get my point. It's mastering inner mindfulness that is the most difficult part. That is why from now on, I want you to do this exercise every day:

Again we will focus on:
1. Seeing
2. Hearing
3. And feeling

But this time, we will scan our emotions and what's inside.

I want you to sit still and focus on breathing in and out.

Just relax for a few minutes. Breathe in and out. Breathe in: mindful, awakening energy.

Breathe out mindless illusions...

Now, this part will be simple and natural for us. Why? Well, it would be hard if I told you to 'just mediate and eliminate all of your thoughts.' Why? Because it's hard to eliminate all of your thoughts. In fact it's not possible at all!

So what we will be doing in this mindfulness meditation is simply scanning and label our thoughts and emotions.

Let's say the first thought that comes to your mind is that you have to do something.

OK, that's fine!

"I have to write this report. I have to write this report."

Now here's the trick. Our mindless mind, also called "monkey mind," will try to come up with all possible scenarios to make us anxious. For example - "I won't have enough time, I will mess up, other colleagues will do it better, I will not get this promotion," and similar.

Here's what you need to do. Get back to the main thought and just stay with it, just like it is.

I have to write this report.

See it, hear it, and feel it. Label it as it is without seeing it too negatively or over-positively. Just see it as it is.

I have to write this report.

When you're ready, focus on the next thought or feeling.

Sometimes it may even be something like:

My belly is digesting my lunch. My belly is digesting my lunch.

I feel grateful. I feel satisfied.

There no real set way to do it. I believe that everyone does it in their own way.

The reason why I write books on mindfulness and what I call holistic self-help is simply to let you know my way. I believe that when trying things out, you will figure out your own process that works for you. My suggestions are merely a starting point on your journey. As I always underline, I am not a spiritual guru, and it is not my intention to become one.

I am your friend, and we are on this journey together.

Practicing Mindfulness in Everyday Situations

What if you don't have time to sit and meditate all day long? Well, this is something I talk about in my other book on mindfulness called "Mindfulness for Busy People" (published in May 2015).

It all starts off with you making a decision to make mindfulness your lifestyle. For example, you can choose to be mindful while commuting to work. Or you can choose to be mindful while doing your dishes.

You can even choose to be mindful when doing certain tasks you don't really enjoy. With mindfulness, you can learn to be passionate about whatever it is that you do. Anything that you know will help you grow personally, spiritually, or professionally.

In this day and age, we are very picky and choosey, and we only what to do the things we love and are passionate about. While I believe that in long term, it makes sense to create your professional path around something you are passionate about. I also recognize the fact that sometimes in order to follow our passions, we must go through certain processes and tasks that we are not really that passionate about. There is a learning curve to everything. This is where many people give up and say 'but I don't enjoy it,' or 'but this is not my passion.'

However, taking a mindful approach and putting the ego down, we may ask ourselves: will doing this task help me live my passion long-term?

Also, the line "just follow your passion" sounds great, but really, if it was so easy, everyone would be happy with their jobs. They would just follow their passions and get paid for it straight away. In this scenario, nobody would ever complain about their jobs or businesses.

However, reality is different. I can honestly tell you that I enjoy what I do, and I do follow my passion. I also believe that mindfully listening to one's gut and asking oneself, "What is my purpose, and how can I provide value?" helps.

But I can also honestly tell you that in order to be able to follow my passion and do what I love, there were many tasks and processes I had to go through, and I wasn't always that passionate about them. I just learned to take a mindful approach and moved forward.

Even now, there are many aspects of my business that I am not passionate about, and even though now I have a team, there are still certain tasks I have to do myself and can't delegate them. I am not always passionate about them, but I know they allow me to focus on the bigger picture and live my passion long-term. In real life, there is always some sacrifice, sweat, and tears. And again, I don't mean to be negative, and not everything we do has to be achieved the hard way. We also need to be open to receiving. But the best use of mindfulness is knowing and accepting your reality first, being honest with yourself, and then trying to look for something good in bad, learning to be peaceful, mindful, and patient, and moving forward. Don't get discouraged from achieving your dreams. You now have mindfulness in your holistic toolbox of self-development!

Don't allow your mind to get lost in negative stories. Look at things holistically, as they are, but always cultivate gratitude and try to be mindfully passionate about the process of transforming your life with every single step you take.

Maybe you want to lose weight or increase your energy levels. The mindful approach could be this: every day, start journaling and stating how you feel and what you want. Then write your long-term vision for how you want your body to be.

Then, focus on the here and now. Write down 3 simple actions that you can take today that will bring you closer to your goal. Just 3, and no more. This could be having a nice salad for lunch, going for a walk or run, or signing up for some healthy cooking classes that you could attend in the evenings and on the weekend. Don't get too carried away. In the evening, journal again expressing gratitude for the fact that you completed your mini goals. This will give you energy and motivation to carry on this process the next day, and then again the next day.

It will make your life easier and will help you transform your mindset so that you can mindfully achieve your goals.

Mindfulness and Honest Self-Love

How to embrace self-love in an honest and mindful way?

Well, let's have a look at this story…

There are two friends, let's call them Ann and Jane. Both are not very happy with their lives, but they pretend it's OK, and if necessary, they fix themselves with medical drugs or go on shopping sprees. They are both overweight and know that they need to change their relationship with food. Neither of them likes their job. They both feel lonely, but never try to meet new people.

Their life continues the same day after day, and they would both like to change something, but still feel stuck to the same old same old. In the evening, they usually go shopping together, buying things that they don't need to impress people they don't even care about.

Sometimes they get drunk with friends, or order fast food and sit on the couch watching TV.

Now, one of the two friends, Ann, decides to change her life. First, she starts attending seminars during the weekends and learns how to work on her motivation and mindset to change things in her life. During those seminars, she meets like-minded people and starts hanging out with them. They all have similar goals. Because of that, she is not able to hang out with Jane as much as she used to, but she still wants to have her as a friend and cares about her. This is why she keeps telling her about upcoming workshops, seminars, or even invites her to lunch with her new friends.

Jane never accepts those invitations. She prefers to stick to her old ways. She believes that Ann is too into herself and doesn't care about her old friends. She feels talked down to even though Ann does not judge her and simply wants to help her meet new people.

Finally, a few months pass by. During those few months, Ann feels empowered to change her nutrition, go to the gym, and lose weight. She transforms her body and becomes really passionate about health and fitness. She decides to carry on her path and become a health coach.

Now she wants to have a passion-based business where she can help other people transform their bodies, embrace self-love, eat healthier, etc.

Of course, such an ambitious goal takes some time to accomplish, and on her journey to starting her own business, there are many ups and downs and a bit of a learning curve as well. But finally, she is transformed, becomes very popular amongst her clients, and is able to quit her job and start her own business.

Jane doesn't like it. She feels attacked. Instead of being happy about her best friend's success, she begins avoiding her and talks behind her back. "Ann is so into herself! She is so stupid. She quit her job, I bet she will be back begging for it. She can't make a decent living from her business! She thinks she is better than others because she lost weight. I bet she is anorexic now and doesn't eat at all, what kind of a life is that?" or:

"She doesn't attend any of the parties we used to go to because she is always busy with her certifications, trainings, and who knows what. I bet it's all a scam and she is giving her money to some charlatans who won't teach her anything. She will be sorry!"

Jane sees a few friends, and they talk about Ann's success and transformation. Other friends' advice to Jane is:

"Don't worry Jane, just love yourself!"

So Jane takes this advice and lives the same way she used to live, but the problem is that her lifestyle is making her even more sick, tired, and depressed.

Now, is this an example of real self-love? Or is it an example of just pretending it's all OK?

Is Jane's lifestyle helping her be happy, or is it just an escape from a reality she doesn't like?

Finally, who is really practicing self-love in an honest, mindful way? Jane or Ann?

Now don't get me wrong, not everyone needs to drastically change their lives like Ann did. If you are happy where you are and it's not damaging your physical and emotional health, it's fine.

But speaking of mindfulness, we need to be honest about what we think and do.

This story shows that what was really happening is that Jane had too much ego to admit she was getting scared of her friend's success and effort.

Instead of admitting to herself where the real emotions were coming from, she felt better accusing her friend of too much ego and not accepting her help.

Jane's definition of self-love was "I will stay where I am" instead of "I will mindfully scan my situation and try to take some positive actions so that I can enjoy better health. I know that if I carry on drinking, doing drugs and eating fast food, I could develop serious health issues, even cancer, and I love myself enough to put my ego down and ask for help because I deserve to learn how to live healthier."

What do you think?

Mindfulness for Ordinary People

Some days will be better, and some days will be worse. Again, this is nothing but your own judgment. Also, remember that practicing mindfulness does not mean that all your problems will magically evaporate and you will start levitating and seeing auras in 7 days or less.

There is a lot of hype out there. The inner mindfulness practice is really working on your mindfulness muscle. The most important thing is to just go ahead and do it. Put your ego down and have faith in the process.

Now, since I have used the phrase, "Just put your ego down," I would like to stop and talk about that too. Why? Well, because I see that there are quite a few misconceptions regarding this phrase, and many of them can be detrimental to our holistic personal development.

Is ego always bad?

Most spiritual books say that ego is bad for our holistic self-growth, and I definitely don't disagree. But I also believe that there is a positive side to ego that, when embraced, can be very beneficial. As always, it's all about mindful balance.

Ego is good if it translates into passion, ambition, flexibility in your approach, drive, and the desire to provide value. Whether you want to provide value to your family and community through your everyday life, provide value to your clients through your work, or provide value to the company or organization you are working for and help them grow. Ego is good if it appears as a hunger for knowledge and growth. Ego is good if it pushes us to expand, stretch, and grow.

At the same time, ego can be destructive if it results in greed, jealousy, and judgment. It's destructive if a person is not flexible and wants to blindly achieve their goals without caring whether or not they will hurt other people in the process. A person with too much ego, even if they're passionate about what they do, is less likely to succeed because they will always focus more on themselves and what they want instead of on what their clients want. The same applies to their personal life. A person with too much ego will find it hard to build up long-lasting and happy relationships.

Too much ego can prevent us from listening. But a mindful person will know how to smartly and mindfully use their ego to result in positive ambition and drive to move forward. This is why a mindful person won't be too scared to reach out for help and ask someone who is more successful for their guidance.

A mindless and egoistic person won't ask for help, thinking they know it all.

They will reject even the best coaches and mentors as charlatans or "total beginners."

They will focus too much on their past achievements and how great they are and will refuse to go on the part of holistic personal development.

How do I know?

I used to be that mindless, egoistical person.

Chapter 5 Mindfulness for Deep Transformation and Long-Lasting Change

It wasn't until I reached the bottom and all areas of my life crashed that I decided to do something about it. Mindfulness was one of the first things I found, and I learned to use my ego in a positive way. I used it to set certain goals for myself to evolve in the right direction.

Mindfulness and Overprotecting Others

Even though I have been practicing mindfulness for a few years now, this is what I recently discovered after doing some deep soul diving. There is always something to learn, and the reason why I am so open about my experiences and imperfections is so that you have some real-life references and examples.

The drive to help others and give them the proper tools to help them on their journey (whether it's health, life, relationships, or career) is a beautiful thing. Don't get me wrong.

However, I have learned that everyone has their own process, and in order to grow and learn, they will, and probably even should, make their own mistakes.

To put it simply, help others when they need it. But don't overdo it because they might think that you don't believe in them or that you think you are better than they are.

I used to lecture people about health all the time, even when they were not interested in listening to me.

Now I take a mindful approach, and instead of just lecturing like "do this, eat this don't eat that thing," I say, "I have been through this journey, and I can always share my experience with you. If you want, or if you are ready, let me know.

Most people hate being lectured unless they ask for a lecture. Even though you are trying to help, they may see it as a personal attack.

Of course, if I see that someone has a serious problem, I will share whatever information I have that can help them solve it, but with mindfulness. I do it in a friendly and non-judgmental way.

Mindfulness and Journaling

If you are ready for the next step, I suggest you go through this journaling exercise.

You can either do it in regards to your life in general, or in a specific area of your life. Then you can repeat the same process to analyze other areas of your life.

Divide a piece of paper into 3 parts.

The first part is called: *What I really mindfully want*

The second part is called: *What I need to mindfully start doing to get there*

The third part: *What I need to mindfully give up to get there*

Unfortunately, the third part is what most people don't like, and I don't blame them. But again, sometimes it's not about what you like or what you don't like. It's just the way it is.

We must accept the good and the bad.

The next step is to take action. But I am not referring just "taking massive action" the guru way.

I am referring to taking meaningful and purposeful action in the right direction to avoid unnecessary stress. And if stress happens again, you will mindfully scan yourself to get to the root of the problem and deal with it in a holistic way. What is causing you the stress?

This is what true self-love is all about. It's not about saying it's OK when it's not OK. It's not about saying "but I just love myself." It's about mindful self-honesty.

Let's say a person does the above-mentioned exercise to improve their health and fitness.

What I really mindfully want

I want a slim body, to be healthy, and have tons of energy.

What mindful actions will I take?

Eat more fruits and vegetables. Learn healthy recipes so that I can still eat ice cream and pizza, but in their healthier, possibly plant-based versions. Move my body more. Join the gym. Be out on my bike more.

What will I mindfully give up?

Eating fast food. Sitting on my couch watching TV. Spending too much time glued to my mobile device when I could go for a walk and listen to a motivational audiobook instead.

OK, so the person is now mindfully revising this plan every day.

Now there are 2 extreme scenarios that can happen. Both can be detrimental and certainly lack mindfulness:

First - the person overdoes everything, such as doing extreme starvation diets and over-exercising to "lose weight fast," and they either get tired and give up to go back to the same old same old, or they get some health issues because everything in overdose is not good for us. I think that makes sense.

Second - the person looks at the plan and rebels against it straight away.

"But I love myself! I deserve my fast food and burgers and ice cream. Who are you to tell me what to do? You are slim because you are lucky, or maybe you are just starving yourself. Healthy eating is boring. I just love myself, and I love my choices, so I am not changing anything." So what can happen is that this person will only put on more weight and eventually can develop some serious health issues. Possibly even cancer.

Both scenarios are bad and totally lack mindfulness.

A mindful person, with the right dose of self-love, is proactive and looks at things as they are in an honest way. They are patient and trust the process. They use their ego to remind themselves of their goals, but put it down to reach out for help and admit that they don't know it all. They will use failure to learn and progress. They will use negative emotions as their feedback to guide them. They will look at more successful people not as objects of hate, but as mentors and inspiration to give them strength to move forward in their journey.

They will not falsely and mindlessly use the very often over-hyped concept of self-love to give up on their dreams before they have even started.

They will mindfully use the healthy dose of self-humor and embrace their imperfections, gradually moving forward, following their own pace.

They will mindfully notice and reward their efforts and celebrate every little success and even every little failure because it is also a step towards success.

This is what I call real, strong, unconditional mindful self-love. I hope this book is providing you with ideas as for how to embrace it.

Mindfulness and Criticizing Others

This was a massive shift for me and making this shift has helped me drastically improve all areas of my health, life, and career.

I used to be very fond of criticizing others and looking at their faults. Until, after diving deep and going through this mindful path of self-development, I realized that I was mostly criticizing myself and my own insecurities.

This was a big truth for me, and I am still on my journey to implementing it as much as I can.

Mindfulness for Anxiety

It usually happens that we focus on what we don't have instead of what we do have.

With mindfulness, we can look at the situation from a different perspective. For example, you may think you don't have or own enough, but for someone else, your life may be the ultimate dream.

There are many countries where people cannot afford to or cannot access methods to order this book. For many of us is it may just be a cheap eBook or a short little book, but for someone else, the cost may be someone's food for a day or even two days. Mindfulness encourages us to think about this planet and its people.

It's not only about us. Thanks to taking this approach and looking at our own problems from a different perspective, we may actually realize that we don't really have so many problems to begin with.

Mindfulness for Laziness

I believe that there are 2 kinds of laziness, and thanks to the process of mindfulness and mindful scans, both can be cured.

The first one is when a person is simply burned out after going through an intense workaholic grind phase. I have been guilty of this, I admit it.

The problem here is not really laziness, even though it may seem that way at first. The problem may be that the person is either physically or mentally tired, or has already achieved their materialistic goals.

In both scenarios, mindfulness can help find two simple solutions. First of all, slow down. Your body and mind need it. Relax so that you can be active and productive again. As a second solution in case a person has lost their motivation, they may want to re-evaluate their goals and shift more to contribution or something that is bigger than them. This will work for people who worked hard to achieve something like a certain amount of money per month, a new car, or a house, and now they have a nice lifestyle but feel like they have lost their drive and passion.

What can help is mindful goal-setting and making your goals super exciting.

Sometimes you also need to ask yourself: Do you need to slow down or take more action?

Sometimes you need to do the opposite of what you think. It's as simple as that.

Now, the second scenario is when a person gets a bit overwhelmed and doesn't know where to start, or maybe they have faced lots of pain and rejection. For example, imagine someone who lost their job and now they are at their parents' house, trying to find a new job and being judged for "being lazy."

Well, what is really happening here is that the person is anxious or depressed. Some people are more sensitive and find it harder to adapt to change. If you are one of those people, accept it and focus on the root of the problem. Embrace mindfulness to stay focused and centered. Don't take on more than what you can. Be sure you journal and start your day with simple and doable actions that will help you move forward. Avoid super-long to-do lists as they will only keep you paralyzed.

Mindfulness and Shiny Object Syndrome

Whatever it is that you are planning to do, whether it's committing to a new healthy eating plan or starting a new business, be sure you commit to one thing mindfully until you get some sort of results that will help you determine whether the given process works for you or not.

You have probably heard about people who go on a different diet every week and buy books on different diets but never actually read them fully.

It's the same with business. I have seen people jumping from one venture to another because they have seen someone making X amount of money with a different business and now they think they should do it too.

However, it's all about focus. Mindful focus. Our attention and concentration span are limited. You can't do it all at once. You may see someone successful with a certain diet program or a certain kind of business, and it may seem like an easy, overnight success. But did you have the chance to see the backstage and all the energy they put into the process? It requires incredible amounts of mindful energy and focus. It's as simple as that.

Mindfulness to Let Go and Achieve Peace

It's not about avoiding negative feelings and escaping from them, but it's also not about dwelling on them.

You know those voices in your head commenting on certain unpleasant situations? Maybe someone was rude to you or you feel that you said something stupid?

You probably know the solution: Just stop indulging in the same inner conversation every 20 minutes.

But the question is: how do you do it? Here's where mindfulness comes handy.

Instead of focusing on what happened and feeling bad about it, it's better to breathe in and out.

Scan your negative feeling from the inside out. You can give it a color and visualize it going away.

At the same time, don't bury it and don't deny it. All of those feeling are feedback.

Mindfulness and Gratitude

Here are my mindful gratitude rules:

Practice gratitude every day, not just on Thanksgiving.

Celebrate life every day, not just on your birthday.

Tell others how much you love them not only during family occasions.

Find joy in giving and receiving all year long.

Don't beat yourself up.

Focus on progress and be grateful for your own pace.

Whenever you're facing failure and adversity, mindfully scan the situation.

State the facts and look for solutions.

Finally, remember...

"When walking, walk. When eating, eat." - Zen proverb

Conclusion

Whatever it is that you are doing is a gift. Why? Because your time here is the most precious asset you were given.

Use this time to mindfully love, breathe, and feel alive. Try to inspire others even if you have a bad day. Many people will resonate with the fact that you tell them that you are not feeling confident or happy. While people don't like constant complainers, it's normal for even the happiest and most mindful people to have a bad day. This is what I call an approach that is both positive and realistic. We all need to dive deep, be more loving, compassionate, and help one another. I believe that mindfulness is an incredible tool, and we can all unleash its power. Keep practicing mindfulness your own way and do what feels right for you.

For more inspiration visit:

www.holisticwellnessproject.com

Grab a free complimentary audiobook at:

www.HolisticWellnessProject.com/mindfulness

Let's connect:

www.facebook.com/HolisticWellnessProject

www.instagram.com/Marta_Wellness

info@holisticwellnessproject.com

Book 2

Holistic Relaxation- Erase Anxiety!

Effective Natural Therapies, Stress Management Techniques, Holistic Remedies, and Wellness Coaching for Busy People

By Marta Tuchowska

Copyright © 2014, 2016 by Marta Tuchowska

www.HolisticWellnessProject.com

Introduction

This book is an overview of the whole variety of solutions to fight stress and anxiety with natural and holistic therapies. You will discover the powerful world of treatments that CAN be an effective solution for a busy, modern individual who needs HOLISTIC relaxation and rejuvenation. You will be able to take control of your life and the way you feel without getting into anxious states or panic attacks that very often come down to unsuccessful stress management or no stress management at all. You will finally discover the new, improved life quality and the long-term benefits of going healthy and reducing stress and anxiety without any chemical medication that might be detrimental to your health in the long run.

I had always been quite nervous and anxious person by nature, however thanks to natural therapies I was able to transform myself, I said 'no' to anxiety and became much more confident. The most amazing thing is that I was once a "seeker" (I still am a seeker and always will be), investigating natural therapies in search for answers and solutions to my own problems. The natural and holistic therapies totally absorbed me, and became my main passion and I became determined to learn everything I could about them. I knew that the more I learned, the more I could help others. Not only did I find the answers I was looking for, but I also decided to make some professional changes in my life and train in natural and holistic therapies as well as in massage therapy.

This is how I embarked on a beautiful journey of self-development and I learned many things about myself and discovered more peace of mind. I would like you to remember that there are no quick fixes or cures in a natural world, whether we talk about natural remedies, massage, yoga, meditation or any other natural therapy, it is also important that you employ your mind and give your treatment a meaning. You need to make a decision and get committed to creating a stress-free lifestyle. If I could do it, you can do it too.

Natural therapies have changed my lifestyle, changed me and changed my focus. I became more aware of what was going around me and eventually I even changed my reaction to many things. I learned how to control my emotions and how to use the natural remedies for an increased zest for life. Moreover, I found my inner peace and focus and I was able to make more drastic changes in my professional life. By doing what I love, which is holistic wellness and personal development, I found even more fulfillment and peace as I was finally able to share my passion with others and make them discover a myriad of natural anti-stress solutions. Once nervous, anxious and totally out of control I successfully turned myself into the opposite. Again, it wasn't an overnight fix. It was hard work that was also fun and it really did pay off now that I think of it. The process of this transformation can be a really enjoyable journey.

The deeper message that I am trying to convey here is that your act of transformation may start right now, with this little book. As you gradually become aware of your body, your mind and your emotions and you also learn to feel and explore the main rule of the holistic world (which is always to get to the root of the problem that your body and mind are encountering), your stress levels will be drastically reduced. This is because while discovering natural therapies, you will also learn a lot about yourself and your way of thinking. Like I mentioned before, I am a really nervous person by nature. I always check if I have everything done and want to have everything so much under control that it oftentimes led me to stress and anxiety. I had to learn to let it go. I had to learn to celebrate the "me alone time". My main challenge was to learn how not to take action (and stop being a control freak) in some cases, as weird as it may sound.

However, a friend of mine gets nervous and anxious because she has many projects to do and does not take action. She then beats herself up that she should have done this and that and her stress levels skyrocket.

Maybe your case is different. Maybe you begin to feel nervous or anxious when people criticize you or don't appreciate your hard work? What I am trying to draw your attention to is that *the root of the problem may be different.* We may have the same symptoms of undergoing a stressful situation, but since we are all different, and so are the roots of our problems, the holistic treatment with therapies like for example homeopathy and Bach Flower remedies will be different.

Now, this book is not only on homeopathy and Bach Flower Remedies.

It is a collection of different Natural Therapies. This is how I divide them into categories to make them easy to understand for beginners:

1-Natural Remedies- like, for example, herbs (phytotherapy). These may be effective for soothing the nerves, help you hit the sack easily and ease digestion. I like using herbal infusions and they are a great caffeine-free solution for stressed-out bodies and minds. However, the problem is that many people purchase herbs and conduct self-medication without consulting a medical/naturopathic doctor or/and an experienced herbalist. If a person is also on a standard medication, both a doctor and an herbalist should be working closer together. Moreover, even if you know your herb and it works for you, you should abstain from any prolonged use. Herbalists usually set up the time of the treatments, when to pause it or when to stop it and possibly re-take it again. Phytotherapy (or herbalism) is a science. In this book, I have included the most common herbs (alongside with their precautions) that can help you fight stress related conditions, but this is only for informational purposes. More on that in the chapter on phytotherapy. In other works- herbs are fantastic, but they're only the tip of the iceberg. In this book, I will encourage you to dig deeper.

2-Holistic Therapies like Homeopathy and Bach Flower Remedies- what I really don't like is when people refer to those therapies as just "some herbs". There are also many people who, even though they label these as natural solutions, talk about them as if they were allopathic medications, for example, you have X condition, you take this remedy, you have Y condition, you take that remedy and it just does not work that way.

Just to let you know that I have nothing against allopathic medicine, I think that allopathic and natural can be combined, the problem is that oftentimes people reject natural solutions when they could be helpful or the other way round; some people reject scientific research made by doctors. I think that in this day and age, we need both.

For example, many people use this "allopathic" approach with natural remedies of all kinds, when they only talk about symptoms, and simply "prescribe" a given homeopathic remedy as if it was a standard medication. Again, this technique is often used by those who wish to self-medicate quickly, at home, and don't want to invest money in a detailed consultation with a homeopathic doctor.

The same applies to the Bach Flower Therapy. Even though it is easier to learn and to apply than homeopathy (the Bach Flower Remedies are only used for problems of emotional nature, whereas the range of homeopathy is much broader and deeper), don't be deluded into thinking that you can just grab some Bach Flower drops at home, mix them and heal yourself in a matter of seconds. Consult a specialist. They will conduct a test, which is fun, because again you will learn so many things about your real nature (very often also bad things, something that we don't want to admit) and it is going to be an amazing journey. From there on, you will know what to do and which remedies to take.

My homeopathic practitioners and teachers always said that homeopathy is safe, which means that it's not exactly like phytotherapy herbs and that there are less contraindications and interactions (but there are some, like in case of all remedies, both natural and standard medical drugs). Again, I don't like when people just put it all on the same shelf, labeled as "just some herbs". For example, if you self-medicate with herbs, there may be some unwanted interactions with other medications, and/or the treatment may go in a wrong direction. In case of homeopathy, if you take homeopathy granules that are simply not for you, it won't do anything. Zero effect or, as many homeopaths would say, "zero vibration".

There won't be any progress with a treatment, but it won't harm you as a pure herb would do. Still, this would be a waste of time and money. Many people say that homeopathy does not work simply because they did not choose *the right homeopathic remedy*. This is why, I always tell people to abstain from self-treatments, unless you are really qualified in any of these fields. But trust me, even a qualified holistic practitioners want to hear the opinion of other practitioners. Why? Because it is always good to have other person observe you and provide you with their honest feedback. Any kind of a holistic consultation is about getting this kind of a feedback from a practitioner and seeing yourself from the outside, in a completely objective manner.

If, on the other hand, you are perfectly healthy and you get exposed to a prolonged homeopathic treatment, especially with strong potency (let's say, something that can help you ease chronic headaches), you may start experiencing headaches. You may actually bring on an imbalance if you use homeopathy when it's not necessary. This is because you give your body certain kind of stimulus when it does not need it at all, as it is perfectly fine. **Homeopathy is not used for prevention; it is not like a vitamin supplement or a natural mineral supplement or something.**

3-Aromatherapy- this natural therapy is relatively easy to learn and to apply at home, also for self-massage, of course, there are some basic precautions to keep in mind, but no worries, it's easy, it's pleasure and it's fun. The aromatherapy chapter will teach you how to mix essential oils safely to create your own anti-stress blends that you can use at home.

4-Manual Therapy/Massage- yes, massage is also an all-natural therapy. There are many kinds of massage. Our Western world is known for the classic Swedish Massage (here in Spain there is a more advanced and enriched form of this massage that also includes a few manipulations from Osteopathy, and it's called Quiromassage, something I trained in and practice combining with aromatherapy, Reiki and some oriental techniques). The oriental world offers many more forms of massage that can be tailored also for emotional and mental imbalances: Shiatsu, Ayurvedic Massages with aromatic oils (again, personalized), Thai Massage. The best thing you can do is to seek massage treatments from an experienced therapist, but I also do acknowledge that not everyone can afford it as much as they would like to. This is why I promote aromatherapy so much through all my books, courses and my blog. You can create your own aromatherapy rituals that will serve you as a wonderful self-massage treatment that you can do daily to achieve holistic wellness and wellbeing. I will teach you all you need to know about self-care and home spa. Again, there will be certain precautions to keep in mind.

5-Traditional Chinese Medicine and Ayurveda- I am really passionate about these two. They offer a range of natural therapies that include nutrition, mediation, holistic self-care with oils and herbs and massage. The Chinese also have their acupuncture that is very effective in treating both problems of physical natural as well as emotional or mental nature. The Ayurvedic and Chinese kingdom of herbs is really complex. Again, I suggest you abstain from self-medication with these herbs especially if randomly purchased on-line from unknown sources. Always make sure you research the brand. You see, maybe a given herb helped your neighbor Becky treat insomnia. However, your source of insomnia will surely be different than Becky's. Remember me and my friend? She gets anxious as she did not take action. I got anxious as I took too much action and took on more than I could handle (hmm...is it called a workaholism?).

I know that some people simply expect a short reference guide with herbs so that they can be their own guinea pigs, but remember, the kingdom of herbs is much more powerful that you can imagine. Did you know that some herbs may even inhibit the effect of contraceptive pills? (St John's Wort herb is one of them, more on that later).

My ophthalmologist is a medical doctor, a homeopath and phytotherapist. She is also a qualified TCM practitioner. By combining medical analysis and holistic treatments (mainly homeopathy), she saved my eyesight when I had severe uveitis attacks that appeared unexpectedly two years ago. The disease manifested itself again after many years (I had it as a kid). The treatment that she designed was something personalized for me and for "my case of uveitis". I met many people on on-line forums and they were asking me for the cure, "what did you take?". I would just give them my ophthalmologist's phone number and a website so that they get in touch with her. There are different kinds of the same diseases (even standard medicine admits it) and there are even more kinds of the reasons why this disease manifests itself. The reasons, or the roots should be addressed first.

To cut a long story short, my ophthalmologist, told me about many cases of people developing not only eye conditions but also health conditions by using certain natural fad herbs that maybe could have been beneficial for them, but were not used in the right doses and proportion. After that I stopped all forms of self-medication, even natural.

Now, even if my ophthalmologist wrote a detailed book on herbs and homeopathy for eye conditions, it would still be for informative purposes only, and you would still need to consult your doses and the course of the treatment with a doctor or a naturopath, or both! This is why I truly admire naturopathic doctors, guys who studied both medicine as well as naturopathy, and combine the two worlds.

6-Holistic Nutrition- you are what you eat. This is what they say and it is 100% truth. The good news here is that unlike in case of herbs, you can "self-medicate with balanced all natural nutrition" and take certain steps to improve your dietary habits, also to descries your stress levels and feel amazing. Preparation is the key. I know what it's like "not to have time for healthy eating". But you know what? It is actually an excuse. I am sorry of this sounds harsh. There is no reason to resort to fast food and convenience foods. You can cook your own nutritious meals and freeze them. You will also spend less money and the end of a day (not enough money is a factor that stresses us all, right?). Toxins, caffeine and mindless eating lead to mental confusion and poor physical health. The chapter on holistic nutrition will give you more tips as for creating your own menu inspired by alkaline and macrobiotic diets. The rest will be up to you. I am not here to tell you what to do, I believe in holistic nutrition that means creating your own way. I will also provide you with a free, complimentary eBook on the alkaline diet and some simple recipes.

7-Energy work- yoga, tai chi, meditation, reiki….you can just pick up what suits you most and commit yourself to first learning a few tricks and then practicing them regularly. This is a skill that you can take with you wherever you go. No one will take it from you, and once you learn it, it's FREE. You can utilize these techniques to bring peace to your mind even during the most stressful day. It all comes down to motivating yourself to actually doing it (yes, I know, it took me a while to get my motivation work for me).

8-All kinds of sports- I always say that physical fitness equals to emotional and mental fitness. This is because when you work out, you set up new goals for yourself to achieve. Then, you feel more fulfilled. If you can do cardio or run up hill and then do it again and again and keep doing it on a regular basis, you gain more real self-confidence. I talk about it in my book: "Holistic Fitness". You can also get rid of negativity and stress. Just sweat it out and even…shout it out! Many people indulge in alcohol, drugs and tobacco and so they put even more stress on their body, mind and emotions. The drug that I have chosen for myself is fitness. I am going to try to motivate you, because even the busiest 21st century individuals can squeeze in 15 mins in their schedules to actually work out, and as I always say: sweat out their tension and anxiety. This will be discussed at the end of the yoga chapter.

9-Conversation- yes, talking to someone is a natural therapy. It may be your best friend or a therapist. Some people feel better after talking to someone they know, some people prefer to confide in a person who is actually a specialist or …a complete stranger. Why? Because someone who doesn't know you, will give you their honest feedback even though it may hurt sometimes, it can also help you open up your eyes and realize where your problems are coming from (tough love they call it!).

10-NLP/Coaching and ...self-coaching- Like I mentioned earlier, if you want to be successful at stress management, you also need to employ the power of your mind. You see, working in the wellness and natural therapy sector, I know many people who simply drop some Bach Flower remedies, take herbal treatments, do yoga a few hours a day and eat super healthy yet....they are still stressed out. The problem is that they are not always willing to take action and commence on a bigger transformation within them. We need to work on our minds as well. It took me many years to realize it.

At the same time, I know guys who don't go overboard with all this "healthy stuff", yet they are balanced and peaceful. My partner is a perfect example of such a person. He doesn't need to take any natural remedies, because he knows how to control things in his mind. I don't know if he was born with this skill or he acquired it. Since his childhood wasn't a bed of roses, and he had to work from a really young age, I think he had to toughen up and he knew how to use it for his own advantage and how to be grateful for this experience. Many people do it the other way round and they see themselves as victims instead. This is why I can proudly say that my boyfriend has mastered this way of thinking that uses a certain shift as how to perceive things and people around him, to turn his childhood experience into a valuable lesson instead of a trauma. He does it intuitively, he has never done any therapy himself and is not really familiar with life coaching or Neuro Linguistic Programming.

This is what NLP teaches us. You have a power to give meaning to certain things, events and circumstances. You can be a victim or you can be an achiever, it all depends on how you interpret what's happening to you.

You got rejected at the job interview. You feel down. Cheer up! See it as an experience, you got more confidence and you will feel more prepared for the next interview that may be actually for a job of your life.

I first studied the human body (I began with nutrition and massage therapy), but I knew something was missing. This is how I got interested in coaching. Through all my books, articles and courses I try to inspire people to become their own coaches. I believe in the concept of self-coaching that will help you shape your new, positive view of the world. So this book, is not just another "natural herb cure guide". While I love natural remedies, we also have some mind-body work to do...

Now you know what I mean by natural mind and body therapies. It goes beyond the traditional natural remedy concept where a person just takes some natural healing fixes and expects a miracle to happen overnight.

All systems must go. Holistic therapies are not only about "taking" natural stuff. It's also about *practicing a holistic lifestyle* and becoming more aware of your body, mind and emotions and how one imbalance affects the rest. This is how I advise you to create your own stress-management program.

I don't believe in the same program for everyone. I believe in providing my readers with information, inspiration and motivation to take action. I also believe in creating. By choosing some of the natural therapies from this book, you will be gradually able to enhance your holistic healing and discover a new, balanced version of yourself. You will also know that some of the therapies, despite their growing popularity, like for example, herbs, are not really designed for self-medication. But, most importantly, you will realize that it all comes down of going to the root of the problem and understanding why you react in a certain way.

Sometimes you have to get exposed to stress in massive amounts so as to finally overcome it. For example, I would get terrified at a mere thought of public speaking. I still do. This is why I try to do it as much as I can. Every time I do it, I feel less anxious. In fact, now it's more excitement that I feel. One thing I certain, I am going to have to do it again and again. How many times? I have no clue. Maybe a dozen, or hundred or thousand. It's just like getting confidence behind the wheel. You will never get it unless you actually drive regularly.

I have decided to create this book, to share my natural therapy knowledge with you and make it as easy for you to understand and to apply as possible. I am a firm believer in simplicity. Life is already complicated enough, right? The methods described helped me, and if you give them a try they can help you too.

One of the reasons why I personally prefer natural therapies to chemical medications is that the natural treatments also address the cause of the illness or imbalance, not only the effect. They also turn out to be much more personalized; homeopathy or Bach flower remedies offer endless combinations to be tailored to each individual case of anxiety or other condition.

Still, remember that <u>I am not a medical doctor</u>. I am not able to give you any kind of a scientific insight or approach. <u>I am not a psychologist</u>. I am simply a holistic wellness coach but I don't reject the standard medicine. I have always believed that natural and standard medicine can be successfully combined- this is my preferred approach. I can guide you through natural therapies, but if you have been struggling with anxiety and depression for a long time I suggest you consult with a medical doctor who also specializes in mental and emotional health.

Ready to immerse yourself in the world of holistic self-care and relaxation?

Let the journey begin!

Disclaimer

A physician has not written the information in this book. Although natural therapies are safe to use, if you suffer from any serious medical condition, are pregnant, or on medication, you should consult your physician first to see if you can apply the natural therapies described in this book. It is also advisable that you visit a holistic health practitioner so that you can obtain a highly personalized treatment for your case. Most of the natural therapies can be safely employed at the same time but it is still always recommended to consult your physician first. **Some homeopathic treatments can inhibit aromatherapy treatments** and vice-versa and some **herbal treatments may inhibit the oral contraceptives**.

The author does not claim that natural therapies can substitute the standard, medical treatment but wishes to provide natural alternatives for anxiety treatments. **She does not claim that reading this book will alleviate anxiety, but offers an overview of alternative and natural therapies that you may find helpful.**

Thanks again for taking an interest in my book. In appreciation, I would love to offer you a free audio book + complimentary guided meditation (audio). Listen to them whenever you feel like you need more peace and balance in your life.

DOWNLOAD LINK:

www.holisticwellnessproject.com/mindfulness

As an added bonus, I will also send you a free copy of my book "Holistically Productive" (PDF and MOBI formats).

If you happen to have any technical problems with your download, email us at: info@holisticwellnessproject.com **and we will help you!**

Chapter 1 Stress- a Blessing in Disguise?

I think that stress or feeling stressed out to some minimal level is not a bad thing as it can motivate us to take action. However, it becomes a nightmare when it alters are bodily functions (insomnia, lack of appetite, binge eating, no sex drive, hormonal imbalances and even hair loss) as well as our emotions (we feel moody, bitchy, can't socialize, can't think logically or confront everyday problems).

In other words, if you feel stressed out beyond comprehension, even a regular trip to the supermarket at the least busy time may feel like a mission for you. And when you get there (driving there will be even more stressful as you will be overacting on the road and shouting at other drivers), you will be freaking out looking for your favorite almond milk brand, even if there's is no line, you will be imagining that there is; and to top it all off, you will be left with nothing as you have left your credit card at home.

This is like a nuclear reaction….and we don't want to end up there. Yes, I know, your colleague, or your neighbor, tells you to relax, or to chill out, but it's not as easy as it seems. Eventually, living in so much stress, can lead to anxiety. Sometimes it may also seem to you that you HAVE TO be doing something and so even when you lie down on your yoga mat, your mind can't relax and starts dwelling on possible problems and work schedule.

You may end up as a bag of nerves and overact to everything that life throws at you. I have been there myself and I know what it's like. I can still remember going to work a few years ago and just shaking for no obvious reason. It just felt like a nightmare. To make things worse, I would always imagine the worst thing happening to me. The problem was also my own mind. I would constantly tell my subconscious that my job was stressful (most people usually complain about stressful jobs anyway), that I was underpaid and that a boss was a horrible person. Now, looking back, I can tell that even though it was not my dream job, the boss was OK, and so were most of my colleagues; it was me who was oversensitive and overreacting, I am actually surprised they could put up with me!

It is just normal for people to become anxious when they are in a difficult or challenging situation. Examples would include taking an exam, a job interview, or even a blind date. But then, there are people whose fears and worries overwhelm them too much that their daily lives are greatly interfered with.

Anxiety is actually a natural response of the body to danger. It is similar to a fire alarm that would sound or make its presence known when the person is facing a difficult or stressful situation. This is why it is normal to feel anxious at times. When in moderation, this is not a bad thing. Studies have even shown that anxiety can help a person to become more focused and alert, as well as motivate a person to come up with solutions to his or her problems. Anxiety also pushes one to do something about the stress-causing situation. However, if the anxiety and high stress levels become constant and overwhelming, when it makes a person unable to function well in various activities and relationships, this is not normal anymore. Chances are that he or she is already suffering from an anxiety disorder.

The different factors that could trigger the onset of anxiety are the following:

Environmental factors

-Stress coming from personal relationships, such as strained marriages, friendships, and divorce

-Trauma from situations like the death of someone they love

-Stress from work, school, financial problems, and even natural disasters

-Lack of sleep, relaxation and balanced nutrition as well as indulging in alcohol, tobacco and drugs make our bodies deprived of minerals like for example magnesium and potassium, this is why we feel fragile, anxious and with no energy levels. In other words, we may feel seriously overwhelmed.

Use and abuse of various substances

It is said that about 50% of patients who are making use of mental health services for the treatment of anxiety disorders like social phobia or panic disorder get treatment because they are dependent on benzodiazepine or alcohol. Anxiety has also been known to be a result of intoxication due to a drug, like amphetamines or cocaine, as well as withdrawal from drugs like heroin or prescription drugs like Vicodin.

Medical factors

There are medically related factors that could cause high stress levels and anxiety, such as infections, heart conditions, stress stemming from a serious illness, and side effects of different medications. This is why natural therapies like Reiki, meditation, acupuncture and Bach Flower Remedies have been gaining more popularity as complementary treatments that can be combined with standard medications to reduce stress levels and help patients relax and heal holistically. All systems must go together: body, mind and spirit.

Genetics

There are researchers who say that family history plays a big role in the onset of anxiety disorders as well as natural ability to cope with stress. If there is a family member who suffered or suffers from anxiety disorder, there are higher chances of another family member developing an anxiety disorder as well.

Both my mom and my grandmother are nervous by nature, as well as prone to anxiety, worrying too much and often panicking. It may seem logical that I inherited some of their "general nervousness", however as soon as I started working on myself via many self-help and personal development courses, seminars, books and programs, I discovered that I can redefine myself. In other words, I stopped repeating to myself that I am a bag of nerves as "it just goes in the family" but I have consciously decided to change my story. This is what I learned from Tony Robbins- one can re-tell and redefine their story instead of using the same one all over again.

I said to myself: As a kid, I would always get flu and colds and everyone would say: "she is always getting ill". This is why I was getting ill. As an adult, I realized how to take better care if myself and I learned all I could about self-care, nutrition, meditation and holistic therapies to apply them in my life. I started going to the gym and made myself strong and fit. And...I stopped getting ill.

If I could achieve it with my physical health, I thought, I can do the same with my emotional wellbeing. Instead of blaming genetics and remaining where I was, an anxious, easily agitated creature, too scared to breathe sometimes; I decided to change my story. I recognized the fact, that even though I may be a "really nervous person by nature" I can also do all I can to TRANFORM MY LIFESTYLE and commit myself to becoming a calm, focused and peaceful person that spreads positivity, wellness and tranquility. Eventually, I started getting compliments from people, as some would say: "Wow, you seem so focused and balanced". This was my new definition!

My main motivation was stemming from the fact that I also wanted to help other people, motivate them and inspire them.

You see, some people were just born with physical strength and high immunity (physical, mental and emotional). Just like some people were born with a natural ability to cope with stress, think calm, and never be a victim of anxiety. Some people, like me for example, had to work hard to get there.

So, even if all your family are anxious, nervous and easily annoyed individuals and you assume that you have this "tendency", you can also take a few deep breaths, move forward, and equip yourself with as many natural therapies as you can to erase stress and anxiety. Just do the best you can. Call it: self-development and self-empowerment work.

Please mind, that I am just expressing my personal beliefs here. You may agree or disagree with me.

The following chapters will discuss the different alternative therapies that could help in relieving anxiety effectively and holistically without drugs. Even if you don't suffer from anxiety, you will learn the basics of natural therapies that you can always apply to increase your quality of life. You may turn to them after a stressful day at work, or during any difficult situation that life may throw at you. We are all fragile human beings, and worry, stress and sadness are imbedded in our human life experience.

Take a few deep breaths again, in and out. Please- do it. Put the booklet down and take a few deep diaphragmatic breaths. This is how you will be able to absorb and learn more from this read. Close your eyes and carry on breathing slowly. Put your hand palms on your eyes. Keep breathing. Finally, when you are ready, slowly open your eyes, stretch your neck and try to remain conscious about your breathing...

Chapter 2 Body and Mind Techniques for Holistic Relaxation

Oftentimes, those who submit themselves to traditional doctors due to stress would get prescribed drugs to alleviate the symptoms. However, these drugs become less effective, especially when used long-term. They also have a lot of side effects. This is why many people suffering from anxiety and stress disorders more often prefer relaxation training. It will also give a very rewarding sensation that you could achieve it by yourself, by simply changing your lifestyle routine.

Personally, I have never used any standard, medical pill treatment for anxiety for nervousness, but many of my friends and clients have. From what I have noticed and from what they told me- instead of helping fight anxiety, the drugs, very often, did the opposite only aggravating the problem. Again, I am not a doctor and I am not making any claims here. I am sure that standard medical treatments are also useful in some cases. I only want to introduce you to natural solutions that will make you feel stronger. You can reduce stress and erase anxiety yourself, natural therapies are the best holistic tools. All you need to do is to make a decision now and stand up for yourself.

Progressive relaxation

This is considered as one of the most commonly studied form of relaxation therapy. All it takes is mentally thinking about the different muscle groups in the body, and then tensing and relaxing each group individually. This is actually a very simple exercise that could be done anywhere. I used to practice it myself when commuting to work (don't do it when driving though!).

With practice you will be able to spot the muscles easier when they feel like they are anxious. It is true that muscles become tense when one is anxious, but many people do not notice that this is a sign of anxiety. Of course, when you do lots of physical activity, your muscles get tense, but usually this is only a physical complaint. Your mind might be peaceful because the physical pain your muscles are going through may be just down to really intense workout. However, as a massage therapist I have had lots of patients (especially when volunteering for an organization that helps homeless people) with anxiety and during massage they would often confide in me and tell me about their problems. Many of them would go really tense just at the mere *thought* of something bad that happened to them, or simply *talking* about big life changes that they were about to undertake and how insecure they felt because of that. Very often they could not control it, or were not even aware of it. Many of them got used to living in constant emotional and physical pain.

Our muscles tell us a lot how we feel. Some people, when under stress, tend to suffer from shoulder pain or lumbar-area pain. What happens to me when I begin to experience stress, is that I get a neck pain. I usually read it as a sign that my body is giving me to slow down. I used to attribute this pain to computer work, but then I realized that I used to work on a PC much more, and never had this pain. The last time it returned was when I was moving houses. It may also appear when I am doing my taxes (stressful). But...I know how to get rid of it, because I have trained my muscles. So, me and my "pain in the neck" would just have this simple conversation:

PAIN IN THE NECK: *hey, Marta, how are you? I am just to let you know that you need to slow down a bit lady. Not that I want to be here, in your neck, I'd rather go on a vacation, so please do me a favor and slow down.*

MARTA: *hey, my Pain In The Neck. Yes, indeed. I need to slow down. I should have done this earlier but I didn't. Thanks for stopping by and notifying me. Relaxing my body and mind now. You can go on a vacation for a long time now!*

This method revolves around the idea that once the body relaxes, the mind becomes clear. To begin with, tell your subconscious that you are the boss of your body and mind. Start giving your mind very clear instructions so that the body obeys eventually, e.g. "My neck muscles are tense but I now give them an order to relax, my body feels lighter and lighter".

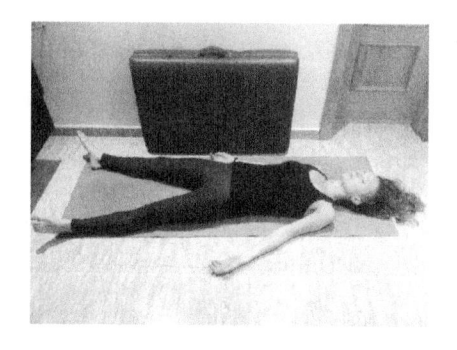

Corpse Pose (Shavasana) is great for progressive relaxation techniques. I especially recommend it if you suffer from insomnia. The more you practice it, the better, as you will become more aware of your body and will be gradually able to control it more than you could imagine. When I suffered from anxiety and panic attacks, my body would just shake and I couldn't control it. I was getting embarrassed about my shaky hands or legs. After learning and practicing this technique I managed to successfully solve my problem and I felt at peace.

Of course, I had to devote time to it. I did not obtain excellent result the first time when doing it. However, the experience I got from practicing it regularly were priceless. I still involve myself in all kinds of workshops, courses, and I do lots of reading to learn more about holistic relaxation techniques. I really enjoy working on a new, confident version of myself as well as getting new tools and techniques to help others do so. Trust me- the world of relaxation never ends.

Autogenic training

This is a technique that could be traced back to the 1930s. It is also used to relax the muscles. This involves repeating a mantra that you must keep on repeating as you go through the different major muscle groups. One could say, "My left arm is heavy," etcetera. The second stage employs the induction of a feeling of warmth in the different muscles. Once one has already made the muscles "heavy" during the first stage, another mantra for warmth is repeated, "my left arm is very warm," etcetera.

The following stages involve calming the abdomen and the heart. . It is a powerful mind and body exercise that can be practiced everywhere; everything starts in our mind, including how we feel physically. This is why if we learn to control it, we will also be able to produce a complete, physical relaxation and reduce many symptoms of high stress levels. The nice sensation of warmth and feeling safe accompanied by regular heartbeat, calm and focused breathing as well as focused mind will be the result of a regular autogenic training practice. You can train your body and mind to do it. You can even do it now. Just lie down on a couch or a yoga mat, and after performing a few deep breaths relax your body with "healing" mantras. Use your imagination. You may even record them on your mobile and play them when you wish.

Here's an example of what you can say/think (by the way, you should not be ashamed of saying these mantras aloud. You can even do it in front of a mirror, looking at muscle groups you are trying to relax):

- I breathe in to provide my body with fuel it needs. Each time I breathe in, my body becomes more energized and less prone to stress. Each time I breathe out, my muscles feel warm and relaxed.
- I breathe in a refreshing, warm air that heals my body and soothes my mind. As I breathe out, I can see a big, dark cloud of all toxins that my muscles expel. My muscles feel lighter and energized.
- I control how I breathe. I breathe in and out slowly and I enjoy the process of relaxing my body and mind.
- People who want to make me feel stressed out and exhausted are not worth my focus. I devote my free time to relax every cell of my body and to nourish it with oxygen of positivity.
- As I breathe in and out, my back and my neck feel warm and relaxed. I can feel a gentle but firm touch of my therapist's hands that heal and eliminate tension. I breathe in and out loving every second of this relaxation treatment. I can smell the softness of massage coconut oil. My muscles feel healed. The tension is evaporating as I breathe out. The coconut oil fragrance is amazing.

Applied relaxation

This technique builds on what was learned from progressive relaxation. However, instead of tensing the muscles, it moves straight into relaxing the muscles. People have to associate using a certain cue to "turn on" a relaxed state. An example of a cue phrase is this: *Serenity, now*! Every time that you feel anxious, he or she can simply say this, and it will trigger the body and the mind to become relaxed. You will then learn how to enter a relaxed state more quickly.

In order to enter this state, I suggest you work with certain fragrances (for example, natural essential oils), colors (you can paint a wall in your house to any soft, gentle color that you associate with relaxation) and music.
Your body and mind will get trained to enter into a relaxed state when exposed to all those visual, auditory and olfactory sensations.

You can also take it to a whole new level. The more you practice it at home, exactly at the same place, with the same music, smells and colors, the more you will be able to practice it outside. Your body and mind will get used to it and so the mere fragrance you used to work with, will make you feel relaxed. When utilizing this technique, I suggest you work with mantras and incantations as much as you can (for example: "I control how I feel", or: "I love my body and I take care of it"). If, after a while you listen to the same song again, your mind will automatically associate it with the rest of the therapies (colors, sounds, suggestions and mantras). You can even sing the song (aloud or in your mind) when you feel stressed (maybe you are just about to start a job interview or an exam). You should feel a nice wave of warmth and peace.

But again, remember, Rome wasn't built in a day. My tip for you is to practice it every day, for about 15- 30 minutes. Your body and mind will be utterly grateful. The ritual can be also combined with some natural, relaxing infusions that will be covered in the next chapter.

Meditation

This method focuses more on the mind compared to the first three methods. It's basically about the 100-breaths technique, which involves breathing in and out deeply a hundred times. Each breath should be counted, which means that you will be more focused on your breathing instead of the situation that causes stress. This is a really simple technique for beginners as well as those who don't have time to meditate for hours. To be honest, I don't think that in order to master meditation, one should be meditating for hours. You can obtain better results if you do short sessions but on a regular basis.

Here is what I do, and it has become my new habit:
-When I wake up, I do the 100-breaths technique; however I try to do it a bit faster, since I want to wake up my body and mind. Oh, and I nearly forgot- smile when you do it. You can also jump when you do it. Jumping is like a natural lymphatic drainage that will help you eliminate toxins from your body.

Toxins are acid forming, and all kinds of acidity that accumulates in our tissues lead to low energy levels, moodiness and makes you prone to stress and acidity. We will talk more about it in a chapter on holistic nutrition and an alkaline diet.

Another reason why you want to jump when doing this technique...

Tony Robbins says that "Emotion is created by motion". So...when you wake up, you want to make sure that you start your day with optimal energy levels feeling great. Most people just crawl out of bed and get their coffee, feeling stressed out about going to work, then they drive or take public transport, feeling stressed again. By feeling stressed, you attract more stress.

If you could wake up every day and do a full, 1 hour meditation, yoga, swimming, Pilates, get a massage, Reiki treatment and what not, this would be our ideal world of relaxation. However, the truth is that in this day and age, no one has time to do it.

This is why, I suggest this really simple technique that will take you 5 minutes to do. You can make it 10 minutes if you want (set up an alarm clock, you may get too much into it, go overboard and be late to work, and this may end up in stress and put you off the whole thing, and I don't want this to happen to you).

So, to sum up, give yourself a gift of getting up every morning, feeling like a warrior and achiever. Get up and start jumping and breathing (with a smile on your face, don't forget about smile!). This is a stress-free zone. You are getting your feet wet in it, and it is your mission to spread the stress-free wellness zone to as many people as you can. Think about it, you are going to be nicer and happier. People will feel it. You will be spreading this energy and someone will benefit from it.

These are just simple ways of relaxing the body and the mind. These could be done almost anywhere and at anytime. Once you have mastered the basic tools, you will be able to experiment and create your own relaxation strategies.

-I like to repeat this technique during the day. Especially when I feel a bit lethargic or there is some event or circumstance that was obviously designed to steal my peace of mind and I don't want to fall victim of it. Some people (haters) are not worth your time, effort and worry. Just let it go. If someone criticized you and it's unfair, don't worry, bad karma will get them eventually. If someone gives you their honest feedback, be grateful for it because you can improve whatever it is that you are doing. These are not haters, these are people who help you grow.

So, whatever little stressor you come across during the day, just give yourself a gift, let it go, don't waste your time even thinking or talking about it. Some things or people are not really worth your nerves. One more thing- something may stress you out, now, today. But in five years you may just laugh back at it. So…if you can, just do it now. Plus, remember about the 100-breaths technique with a smile on your face. New, stress-free you. Repeat this simple technique throughout the day.

Stress-free wellness zone!

If you suffer from any serious medical condition, do not perform this breathing technique (especially in a fast manner) without consulting a physician first.

VARIATIONS OF 100 BREATHS TECHNIQUE:
1. Breathe in through your nose and breathe out through your mouth.
2. Breathe in and out through your nose. It may help especially when you feel angry. When you just begin with this technique it may be a good idea to intervene it with normal breathing, for example you can do 3 sets, 30 nose in and out breaths each, and between each set

breath in and out the regular way (still remember to make it deep and diaphragmatic).
3. Breathe in and out through your mouth. This is what I learned from my Reiki teacher. It's called: "chakra breathing". When you do this technique, you may feel certain blockages, for example in your solar plexus. By carrying on, the tension will be gradually relieved. It also helps clean and balance your chakras and energy field. Again, use your abdominal muscles. You can learn more about Reiki from my book: "[Reiki and Reiki Meditation](#)".

Before I go to sleep, I also do my breathing exercise. I very often fall asleep before I actually finish it! I usually play a nice and soft meditation song, or a play list that lasts no longer than 15- 20 minutes. I lie on my bed and the only thing I focus on is to breathe in and out. By the time my playlist comes to an end, I am already sleeping like a baby.

I used to be addicted to my iPhone and would always reply to my friends or clients immediately, even at midnight. Finally, I realized I was falling victim to technology. I would wake up the next morning feeling tired and naturally craving a cup of coffee and then another, making my body jittery and shaky. The smallest stressor that would appear would just make me hit the roof. This was a vicious cycle that is luckily over now.

I have gotten into the habit of switching my iPhone and other devices at certain time in the evening, usually around 6PM. In your case, it does not have to be 6PM, it may be 4PM, or 9PM; it's up to you, your schedule and your lifestyle. I am not telling you what to do, it's just what I do. The key concept it to know your time to disconnect and go offline so as to focus on yourself and your healing.

Here is an interesting fact about being always available for phone calls, e-mail and instant messages. Again, this is my own personal opinion, but all the people I mention this to, agree with me.

There is a big difference between helping other people and letting other people steal your time and stress you out. Learn how to distinguish between the two. Some people only care about their own business and don't respect your time at all. They don't even want to be helped. Think about it and make your own conclusions. Just observe...

So, to recap, these simple breathing exercises can be done throughout a day, even if you are the busiest person in the world. In the morning, they will put you in a good mood and make you feel confident and powerful. You will also be able to skip or at least reduce caffeine drinks (more on that in the following chapters). Whatever stressor you encounter during the day, turn everything off, just ignore it and focus on yourself. Make your mind peaceful. You see, very often we perceive situations as stressful, because our mind is not focused enough.

This is why we may imagine a storm, whereas it can be an absolutely lovely day with a blue sky at the same time. I hope you get this comparison.

In reality...Everyone is different, we are talking about natural therapies here and natural therapies will never prescribe the same treatment for everyone (let's leave it to pharmaceuticals). Instead, natural therapies only want you to help you get to know yourself. Only you can do it, you are the master of your body and mind...

MEDITATION

When it comes to meditation- I am not a "spiritual meditation guru". However, since I practice it daily in my very own way, I think I can call myself a "do-ru" because I do it on a regular basis. I simply discovered it as a great tool of myself and so I started applying it and experimenting. I am sure that there is something that you can learn from me, but at the same time, if we meditated together I am convinced that I could also learn something from you. Everyone does it in a different way, that's the beauty of it.

I have decided to provide you with a simple example of how I do it and trust me: I am absent-minded and hyperactive by nature. Still, I can meditate my own way.

FIVE SENSES DEEP MEDITATION TECHNIQUE

There are many kinds of meditation and my favorite one is five senses meditation: as the name suggest it requires using your five senses and so you concentrate and focus so much that you connect with your mind. One of the simplest techniques that I recommend is choosing some pleasant moment from your childhood, something that can make you feel well taken care of as well as totally safe, careless and free. It's about releasing positive emotions that immediately relieve the sense of emotional wellness and wellbeing. This is an example of how it can be done; feel free to experiment with your own meditation:

Sit comfortably and breathe in deeply. When you are ready, try to evoke a place or an image from your childhood that you really loved and that brings positive memories and associations. I will give you an example of how I do it so that you can adjust it and make it working for you:

-I imagine a kitchen at my grandma's place. First of all, I focus on the colors and all the visual sensations, anything that I can remember. I just scan the walls, the drawers, the cooker, even the calendar on the wall.
-I then go to the window and have a look at the city. I can see the sky, the trees, the cars, the people, the trams even the rest of the snow on the sidewalk. I take my time to enjoy the view. I try to evoke all the details. There is another block of flats just at the opposite side of the street, and I can even see the colors of the curtains in the windows and bicycles in a few balconies. I already feel peaceful!
-I then start smelling the dinner that my grandma is making for me and the wonderful cake and other fragrances that I associate with being taken care of and stress-free. I open the fridge and all the cupboards and take different foods and items from there and smell them: the coffee, the herbs, and the spices. There is also some home-made bread. I take all the fruits and smell them. The cupboards have an amazing smell of cookies and spices and teas.
-Then I focus on the sounds around me: the sounds from the streets, my grandma and my grandpa talking, the TV, the boiling water, even the birds singing...I can hear the trams passing down the street. This is a city center in a really big city. I can hear all those noises from the kitchen and I like it. I am happy the school is over and I am here on a vacation. The living room is peaceful though. There is a balcony overlooking a tree and there is also a playground. I can hear the birds signing and other kids playing. I know I will be joining them soon.
-I then start tasting the delicious pancakes that my grandma prepared for me. They are creamy, and sweet and made with love. I eat them slowly and analyze the taste of each and every ingredient...I taste the juice and other things that were prepared

especially for me…There is a raspberry marmalade and it is a bit sour but I like it, it composes well with sweet pancakes. Finally, I drink tea with lemon. I add some honey to it to make it sweet. My grandfather gives me some chocolate that I devour immediately.

-Now it's time to experience the sensation of touch…I go to the bedroom and decide to have a nap. My body feels heavy and relaxed after a nice meal. I fall on the bed and can feel the softness of the mattress, the cushions and the blanket…They are really soft and smell of lavender. I keep breathing and relaxing, I close my eyes and focus on the wonderful smell of lavender…

Try this go-back-in-time technique and use all your senses to experience a really magical sense of relaxation and wellbeing. Create it for yourself. You can also invent a situation that will make you feel relaxed. For example, you can imagine that you are on the beach or in holistic spa and your body and mind gets treated. Visualize an amazing place where you are the main character. Use all your senses to "be" there.

You can use this technique everywhere, simply take it with you and ask it to work for you.

Meditation-Additional Resources (Free Audios Included, no opt-in required, you can just download them):
www.holisticwellnessproject.com/blog/mindfulness/meditation-for-bad-days/

www.holisticwellnessproject.com/blog/mindfulness/meditation-how-to-meditate/

HOLISTIC WELLNESS
PROJECT
TOTAL BODY AND MIND TRANSFORMATION

Chapter 3 Phytotherapy for Stress Management

Phytotherapy, or otherwise known as herbal medicine, is a type of specialization where medicinal plants are utilized to treat different health conditions. This is considered as the oldest in the field of medicine because various ancient civilizations employed herbs and plants to get various health benefits.

In other words, when you sip on your chamomile or mint tea because you want to address some digestive issues or to relax, you are using phytotherapy. Instead of relying on a chemical, medical pill, you choose a cup of chamomile infusion to ease the process of digestion. At the same time, you go for a natural solution that is not poisoning your body and also helps it relax as this is what chamomile does. I am a big fan of using natural remedies as much as possible, but of course, I also admit that it's not always possible and that sometimes standard medication should be used.

The problem is that nowadays, people resort to standard medications even if the common complaints they suffer from could be alleviated by a balanced lifestyle and natural therapies. I very often think that what is called "Health care" could actually be called: "Sickness care"; they do care of sickness and its symptoms instead of trying to restore balance to achieve vibrant health. The holistic lifestyle however, prefers to take care of health so as to prevent sickness and imbalance.

Herbal medicine is still considered as the closest counterpart of modern medicine as it has active elements that have certain effects that are specific and well defined on people. However, it is also different because the effects that are seen in a person are due to the sum of the different elements present in the plants instead of just a single active ingredient that has been isolated, as in the case of synthetic medication. Professional phytotherapists very often prescribe specific blends so as to achieve the perfect synergy of different plants and herbs for effective treatments of different kinds, both for physical as well as emotional imbalances.

Nature offers a vast amount of natural remedies for stress and anxiety alleviation. Let's dive into the most common ones that are very often used for anxiety treatments and relaxation. Just like in case of standard medication, there is always a doses and time of the treatment that may be different for me and different for you.

St John's Wort (Hypericum perforatum)

Other common names: *Tipton's weed, rosin rose, goat weed, chase devil.*

- St. John's Wort is known to be an effective anti-depressant. It is capable of inhibiting certain neurotransmitters found in the central nervous system from wreaking havoc in the body.

- It increases the secretion of melatonin at night, which then helps regulate the circadian rhythm.

- It also has a sedative effect and is also widely employed in stop smoking treatments, compulsive eating treatments, and seasonal affective disorder.

Precautions

- Even though natural, St John's Wort may interfere with some medications, including some contraceptive pills. If you are on any medication I advise you consult a medical doctor or a naturopath before you start St John's Wort treatments.

- This herb is available as nonprescription, over-the-counter treatment and so many people take for granted that they can self-medicate, which I don't recommend. Aside from possible counteractions with other medications, the problem is that when not used in precise measurements and doses (it differs depending on a person), it can actually aggravate the problem and make you feel more anxious or even depressed. Personally, I have seen a few friends conducting such treatments without consulting an experienced specialist and the result was that there was no progress or they felt worse. I suggest you mention this herb to your holistic practitioner and physician and to it the right way.

- Possible side effects (especially if not used with caution): gastrointestinal symptoms, dizziness, tiredness and sedation

Not recommended for:

- People suffering from bipolar disorder and people suffering from major depression
- Abstain if you are on medication, unless approved by your physician

Nowadays, it is normally taken in capsules filled with its powdered plants or in tablets, which makes it easy to be employed, and it doesn't require any complicated rituals, like for example preparing certain herbal infusions.

From my own experience: I have tried this treatment a few years ago when I suffered lots of stress because of moving to another country. I took St John's Wort in capsules and the treatment took about 2-3 weeks (can't remember exactly now). I felt calmer and more focused and it helped me get back on track with other therapies, for example yoga and healthy nutrition. You must admit that when you feel anxious or unmotivated it's really hard to take action. I believe it's a good idea to resort to natural herbal treatment that can help us achieve peace and the rest of transformation can be done without taking anything (even natural remedies). My main goal is never rely on any remedies, even natural. I prefer to rely on my own mind and its power, but, hey...we all go through hardship sometimes and we might need some natural "push" to help us restore balance.

More uses:

Not only is it used for depression and anxiety disorders but also physical conditions like: migraines, fibromyalgia muscle pain, sciatica. Some researchers also claim it can ease menstrual cramps and PMS.

Passion flower (Passiflora)

- Passion flower is usually used to depress the autonomous nervous system, which is the one in charge of the heartbeat, peristalsis, and more.

- It can offer a natural relief to people suffering from anxiety symptoms of a more physical nature, like: shaking, increased heartbeat, muscle spasm, feeling suffocated, feeling hyperactive, not being able to fall asleep and excessive perspiration.

Important precautions:

- Do not use in pregnancy. When breastfeeding, consult your physician first, its safety for breastfeeding women is still being researched and speculated.

- If you are already on any kind of medical treatment for anxiety, or other medication- abstain from using passion flower unless consulted with your doctor. This herb has really strong properties and may interact with standard medication.

- The excessive intake of passion flower may result in excessive sleepiness. It is also important not to use the blue passionflower; it's the same family but has different properties and is not suitable for anxiety/stress disorder treatments.

- Even though passion flower is not a strong pain-killer on a physical level it can be a very powerful calming remedy for the mind. Some people may experience a bit of mental fogginess after overdosing this herb. This is why it is important to consult your case with a naturopathic doctor or a qualified herbalist. Unlike standard medicine, there are no equal doses for everyone, especially if mental or emotional problem is to be treated.

- If you are planning a surgery, remember that this passion flower remedy might increase the effects of anesthesia and other medications during and after surgery (it can affect the central nervous system). It is suggested to stop taking passionflower at least 2 weeks before a scheduled surgery, or even better- consult your doctor.

From my own experience: I have tried this herb a few years ago as I had lots of stress in my old job. However, I have made a mistake of self-medicating myself with passion flower in capsules (I followed the instructions that the manufacture attached, but I guess they were not for me), as a result I only felt sleepy for a few days, which actually made things worse and so I gave up. I then repeated it when suffering from insomnia, but I did consult with a phytotherapist. One learns from one's own mistakes, but I don't recommend you do it the way I did it. Better get it right the first time.

Other uses:

- It can be applied topically onto the skin (as an infusion) for burns, and pain and swelling (inflammation).

Valerian (Valeriana Officinalis)

- Valerian is a very popular remedy for insomnia and it has been found to have sedative properties to the central nervous system. It possesses hypnogenic abilities that help people fall asleep, and it also has a muscle relaxant effect.

- An interesting fact about valerian is that in some individuals in may actually bring a totally opposite effect: instead of calming down it may actually turn out to be quite stimulating. This is what happened to me, this is why I abstain from taking Valerian. Luckily, there are not too many cases like mine to be reported and the majority of the people using valerian report an immediate relief. If you find that valerian is not for you, use another herbal medicine then. The wonderful thing about herbalism is that it offers an unlimited number of solutions for different conditions. Valerian can be taken as an herbal infusion however its strong taste and odor is something that many patients get put off with. If that's your case, choose valerian tablets or capsules. Make sure that you research the brand and in case of prolonged treatments you should definitely consult with a specialist.

Other uses:

- Valerian is also used for hysterical states, excitability, fear of illness (hypochondria), PMS and joint pain

Precautions:

- Some people report reactions such as headache, excitability, uneasiness, and even insomnia (like I mentioned, this herb does not really work for me).

- Abstain from using when pregnant (it's better to stay on the safe side, there are different opinions about using valerian in pregnancy, but I would suggest not taking any risks here).

- It may inhibit anesthesia and other standard medications. Definitely not recommended before, during, and after surgery.

Hawthorn Berry (Crateagus Oxycanthus)

- Hawthorn is considered effective in alleviating various states of anxiety due to its ability to have a sedative effect on the heart rate and the nervous system.

- It is capable of decreasing the feelings of anxiety plus vertigo.

- It is also a good remedy for insomnia.

- It is rich in vitamin C and antioxidants

- Helps improve digestion

- Widely used in Traditional Chinese Medicine

Other benefits and uses:

- It is used to lower the cholesterol levels and it is recommended for menstrual cramps as well as indigestion.

- It is considered to be a very powerful antioxidant. Some alternative health practitioners recommend it to help recover the natural alkaline balance of the body and speed up the process of detoxification.

Precautions:

- As in case of other above-mentioned remedies, if you are on medication, consult with a medical or naturopathic doctor as hawthorn may seriously interfere with other treatments (both natural and standard).

- Abstain from using when on medication such as Digoxin or Phenylephrine

- Possible side effects include: agitation, shortness of breath and dizziness.

- Do not use hawthorn berry if you suffer from low blood pressure or any heart disease

Note on herbal medications and regulations- note that different countries may have different policies and regulations on phytotherapy treatments. I am writing from Spanish perspective as this is where I am currently residing. Phototherapy is really popular here and there are many naturopathy consultations available and more and more people resort to it. Still, these are considered alternative/complimentary treatments and are not usually prescribed by doctors. No matter where you live, it is your responsibility to tell your doctor about any herbal or natural treatments that you may be undergoing.

Some European countries, as for example France, include herbalism, aromatherapy and aromatology (also called aroma-phytotherapy or scientific aromatherapy) in their mainstream healthcare and these treatments are also prescribed by doctors (alongside with homeopathy). Sounds great to me!

MORE NATURAL HERBAL SOLUTIONS

There are now a lot of herbal supplements that have a mixture of these herbal remedies, and they have been found to be useful for the treatment of various anxiety states, as well as light to moderate bouts of insomnia. Replacing coffee, black tea or any kind of caffeine drinks or energy drinks with those delicious and calming herbal infusions can bring a body and mind relief and help you feel more relaxed on a physical and mental level. At the same time, these infusions won't make you feel too sleepy or sluggish like for example valerian can.

If you are looking for delicious herbal drinks to help you soothe nerves, or you want to reduce/eliminate your intake if caffeine (which is actually stressing out your body and mind), I suggest you resort to herbal infusions. These already come in tea bags, are generally safe to use at home and can be a part of your meditation rituals from the previous chapters. They also have big amounts of antioxidants which help reduce stress and alkalinize your body. Caffeine drinks on the other hand do the opposite; they create an acidic environment in your tissues and lessen the body's natural ability to heal and restore. It is my guess that you picked up this book to reduce stress in your life, this is why I advise you to quit or at least reduce caffeine as it is a stimulant and a stressor that does not bring you closer to your holistic relaxation goals that you have set up for yourself.

1. **Roibosh tea**
    - Virtually caffeine free and rich in antioxidants
    - Rich in calcium, manganese, fluoride (strong bones!)

- Nice, sweet taste. I usually take it with some almond milk
- Can be taken even before bedtime
- Important: Avoid if you are undergoing chemotherapy (consult with your doctor first) and if you have any existing liver or kidney conditions.

2. **White tea**

    - Antioxidant
    - Prevents cancer
    - Stimulates weight loss, youthful skin and hair
    - It does contain some minimal amounts of caffeine, so avoid if you are caffeine sensitive

    CAFFEINE LEVELS IN WHITE TEA:

    28 mg caffeine per 8 fl. oz cup

3. **Chamomile tea**

    - Antidepressant, nervine, sedative, digestive, relaxant
    - Can help you enjoy better sleep. I love a cup of warm chamomile tea with some almond milk at bed time!
    - It reduces menstrual cramps
    - Caution- some people are allergic to chamomile.

4. **Rosemary tea (*Rosmarinus officinalis*)**

- Antioxidant
- Digestive
- Helps prevent colds and cough, I like to drink it during winter time
- You can also use it as a hair tonic to stimulate hair growth (scalp massage)
- Precautions: avoid in pregnancy, rosemary may interfere with some pharmaceutical drugs like blood thinners.
- I suggest you get it in tea bags and stick to the safe doses recommended, in case of any serious condition you may be suffering from, pregnancy or medication, consult your doctor first

5. **Yogi tea**

    - There are various blends of yogi teas available.
    - The one that I recommend is a mix of:

      -licorice

      -cinnamon

      -burdock root

      -ginger

      -dandelion

      -fennel

      -anise

      -juniper berries

- coriander
- cardamom
- black pepper
- parsley
- sage
- clove
- turmeric

- It is said to assist you in your mediation efforts and connecting with the moment, it is also a digestive and antioxidant drink.

- Make sure you use caffeine free blends and get acquainted with possible precautions, for example, if you suffer from hypertension, you should avoid licorice in large amounts.

- My observations: it helps me feel calm but focused and alert at the same time. You may have noticed that I am a big fan of almond milk...yes, you're right! I have my Yogi Tea with some almond milk in it. In the summer, I like to have it chilled as a smoothie. Here's the recipe:

Recipe***Yogi Tea Style Sweet Smoothie

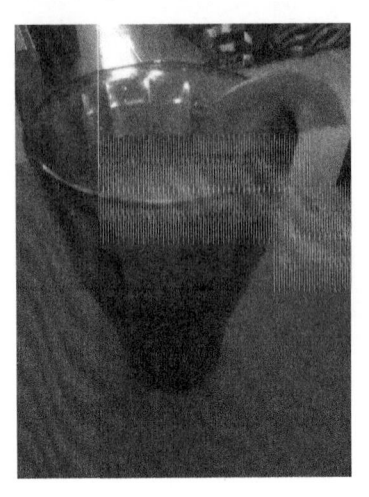

Ingredients (Serves:1-2)

- 1 cup of cooled yogi tea
- 1 banana
- 1 cup of frozen blueberries
- 1 cup of raw almond milk
- 1 teaspoon of cinnamon powder mixed with ginger powder
- A couple of teaspoons of coconut oil

Instructions:

1. Blend and enjoy!
2. You may add a couple of ice cubes and garnish it with a lime slice

3. This smoothie is a great, natural source of Magnesium. You need this mineral to focus better and be less prone to stress.

6. Lemon balm (*Melissa*)

- Helps fight insomnia and provides deep relaxation

- Caffeine free

- Reduces pain (menstrual cramps, headache)

- Used for mental disorders such as anxiety, hysteria and melancholia

- Precautions: while some resources say it is safe in pregnancy, other say it is not, I suggest you remain on the safe side and avoid it when pregnant (unless your herbalist and doctor state otherwise), not recommended to use when a person is on medical tranquilizing drugs, it may interact with CNS depressants, if overdosed Melissa may cause dizziness and sleepiness (abstain from driving).

7. Mint Tea

- Refreshing and energizing

- Stimulates digestion

- Helps soothe headaches and menstrual cramps

- It is generally safe when not overdosed
- Precautions: it may interfere with some liver medications as well as medications that decrease stomach acid

8. Kukicha Tea (Three Year's Tea, Twig Tea)

- Rich in antioxidants
- Almost caffeine free (25 mg caffeine per 8 fl. oz cup)
- Very alkalizing and recommended by alkaline diet and macrobiotic diet followers; in fact, it was George Oshawa, the founder of the macrobiotic diet who brought this tea from Japan to North America
- It is rich in a myriad of minerals: Zinc, Selenium, Copper, Selenium, Manganese, and Fluoride
- Tastes great with rice, coconut or almond milk. This tea served me as coffee replacement; it is a naturally energizing drink that won't make you feel nervous, anxious or jittery. So...keep it calm!

AYURVEDIC COFFEE

Another recommendation I have is entirely caffeine-free Ayurvedic Coffee

- If you are really struggling to commence on your caffeine-free lifestyle, it can help you make a transition and detoxify your body at the same time. The one I recommend is called Raja's Cup. It is a bit bitter, but again, a bit of rice or almond milk and cinnamon gives it a marvelous taste.

- Its ingredients include: licorice (consult your doctor if you are suffering from hypertension, even though this particular coffee blend does not contain high levels of licorice, it's better to stay on the safe side), winter cherry, senna sophera, and clearing nut tree.

- If making coffee in the morning is a ritual you can't miss, then this coffee, or any similar, natural one, may be a product you are looking for!

My tip: reduce or eliminate caffeine drinks. Choose drinks with healing properties instead and take care of your inner peace.

Chapter 4 Homeopathy and Bach Flower Remedies

Homeopathy is a branch of natural, complimentary or alternative medicine first created at the end of XVIII century by Samuel Hahnemann. Homeopathy believes that illnesses and diseases can be cured when you make use of various elements that could cause the diseases that they are trying to get rid of. Instead of using these elements in large amounts, they are diluted so that the amount may no longer cause the disease. The body is then able to take the elements, and the molecules help the body to fight off the disease.

This is believed to be a lot more natural and safer compared to modern synthetic medications and even some of the herbal medications. In other words, homeopathy can't harm you, but it must be used with caution.

It is always recommended to book a consultation with a homeopathy doctor or practitioner. They will probably ask you some very detailed questions about your general lifestyle, certain habits, emotions and even food preferences. The consultation can take even more than one hour so that a homeopathy practitioner can determine which homeopathy medication will work out for you as well as which potency to go for and how long the treatment should last. To make the homeopathy treatment effective, you should stick to your practitioner's guidelines rather than self-medicate with homeopathy. Nowadays there are many natural remedies available on-line and they are labeled as homeopathy but the truth is that many of them are not homeopathy, but phytotherapy, and should never be used as means of self-medication.

To make it simple: let's say that we both suffer from anxiety, even if the symptoms are the same, my anxiety will be still different than yours. This is because we are different and so the internal factors that triggered our anxious states, were different too. Homeopathy addresses the causes rather than the symptoms. Since our causes are different, the treatment will be different. Only an experienced homeopath can "guess" which remedy will work for you.

If you have never heard of homeopathy, or never tried it, let me tell you one thing- it helped me cure my eyesight. This is why I am so passionate about it.

Here are the commonly used homeopathic remedies that help fight stress and even anxiety. One more thing- there is no real scientific proof behind the world of homeopathy. I will leave the judgment to you. You can try it to see if it works. I am a big believer in homeopathy and as I mentioned earlier, it helped me cure me eye from uveitis. It opens a gate to a whole new world of holistic healing as well as can even make you think outside the box. Not everything has to be scientific. Besides, I agree with doctor Robert Young, when he mentions in one of his books (the "Ph Miracle Series") that oftentimes there is no "scientific proof" because it is of the highest interest of some pharmaceutical companies that it remains so…Again, I will leave it to you and your own beliefs. But don't reject it even before you have tried it.

Now, let's get acquainted with a few rather complicated homeopathic names…
By the way, homeopathic remedies all look and taste the same…white granules with sugary taste. This is why so many people are skeptical about it. After all, when it comes to herbs, they are always different, they taste different and the smell is different. The same with aromatherapy essential oils. Then, how come it can

work for a whole range of aliments both of physical as well as mental and emotional nature?

Well...in this world not everything is always cut and dry...However this chapter may be a beginning of something new and incredibly healthy and balanced in your life.

Argentum nitricum- it may be a remedy for you if the following description matches your physical, mental, and emotional state. Of course, it's never set in stone, this is why I suggest you'd better consult it with a homeopath. Still, I think it may be interesting for you to do some homeopathic brainstorming...

- anxiety, dizziness
- general physical and mental lack of balance and focus
- loss of control, urge to balance everything constantly
- shaking, cravings for sweets
- suffering from irritated mucous membranes
- inflammation of the throat
- explosive belching sensation
- can't stand heat
- gets sensations of sudden pinch
- prone to premature ageing
- the condition gets worse when eating cold food, after eating sweets (even though always craving them), women who are

Argentum nitricum experience aggravating their condition when on period or experiencing negative emotions.

If a given description sounds like you, it means that it could be your alleviation. I know that it reads really weird, especially if this is your first time learning about homeopathy.

Let's continue with the rest of homeopathic medications used for anxiety and stress management...

Aconitum napellus
- fear, anxiety
- the sensation of restlessness both mental, emotional and physical
- does not like massage or getting touched
- prone to acute fevers
- feels tense when exposed to cold air drafts, cold and dry climate and very hot climate
- their condition gets worse when smoking, inhaling tobacco smoke
- likes open air, feels better and it alienates his or her condition

Arsenicum album –is used for hypochondriacs, anxiety due to fear of losing one's self-control, as well as death. Here are general characteristics of Arsenicum album people/physical mental and emotional states:
- debility,
- always very thirsty
- fright and worry
- prone to fever

- exhaustion, even after gentle and non-strenuous exercise
- the feeling of restlessness that aggravates at night time
- gets better with warm and hot climate and warm drinks, gets worse when exposed to cold air and wet climate, cold drinks aggravate their condition

Natrum muriaticum:
- Prone to fever, anemia
- Suffers from digestive track issues and skin problems
- Feels weak, especially in the morning, when getting up of bed
- Gets colds very often
- Mentally and emotionally prone to influences
- Prone to diabetes and hyperthyroidism
- Feels better when in open air or using cold baths
- Benefits from irregular meal patterns
- Gets worse when exposed to noise, heat, people talking and warm spaces

Gelsemium –is used for the alleviation of chills and hot flushes due to anxiety. It can also help, if you are feeling nervous before a particular event, for example, public speaking or a job interview. I have tried it myself a couple of times and it worked, I felt more secure. Some friends of mine who are skeptics would tell me that it was a placebo effect. To be honest, I don't care what it was, even if it was a placebo effect that worked, I am grateful that it helped me manage stress in that given moment and do well in my exams. We sometimes put lots of emotions and ambitions in the whole process of achieving our goals. I guess you know the feeling- it can be stressful!

Below are the characteristics of *Gelsemium* type people:

- prone to dizziness, drowsiness
- trembling and shaking
- mental apathy, feeling tired
- weak muscles
- poor circulation
- scared of falling (especially children)
- feels better in open air and after urinating
- gets worse before a thunderstorm or when excited and nervous (can't think clearly)
- can't stand damp weather

A lot of homeopathic remedies are specially made to treat specific stress situations, anxiety disorders, or imbalances that may have caused anxiety and even depression. They may also be used for specific situations, for example, natrium muriatium is used for people who avoid social situations or are shy.

Homeopathic remedies, if chosen correctly according to your case, are believed to take effect right away. It is important, however, to check that the dose is correct, as each individual may have a different dosing requirement.

I am sorry if I am too repetitive here, but as an avid homeopathy supporter I always try to make it clear that it is actually impossible to prepare the same list of homeopathic remedies for everyone, even though their symptoms are the same. The reason for that is that homeopathy centers more on the cause of the illness rather than only the symptoms. The wonderful thing about homeopathy is that if a homeopath is able to choose your homeopathic remedy and design a treatment suitable for you, the cause of your anxiety will be eradicated, resulting in a truly successful treatment. It can also have many other benefits on a physical and mental level and restore overall balance and health.

Even though many medical experts object to homeopathy saying that it doesn't work or that 'there is no scientific proof' to it, there are many clinical cases that speak for themselves. I am actually one of them. Homeopathy saved my eyesight; as a child I suffered from severe attacks of uveitis, which is a very serious condition that can even result in permanent vision loss. Not everything can be measured or described scientifically, but the results still can be seen, touched and experienced.

The reason why it is so effective for anxiety, depression, and even addictions or more serious mental disorders is that homeopathy is a truly holistic therapy and homeopathy practitioners dedicate a serious amount of time to get to know their patients and get a 'map' of their current mental, physical, as well as emotional wellbeing, and use their knowledge to pick one or more homeopathic remedies out of dozens. They will also know the exact potency of the remedies to be employed, as well as duration of the treatment.

There are two schools of homeopathy:

-The Classical School works only with one remedy at a time
-The Complex School of Homeopathy works with more remedies at a time

I have personally found both approaches to be effective. From my experience, the Classical School has proven effective to help me treat problems of more emotional or mental nature (including anxiety) whereas the Complex School was able to help me treat problems that had more physical nature and symptoms, including the above-mentioned eye problems.

Of course, do not interpret it as a rule; it's just what I have noticed from my case as a homeopathy patient.

Homeopathy remedies in forms of tiny, sweet granules (they always taste the same, no matter what remedy you take) as well as liquid drops are a therapy that is very easy to be used, even if you travel.

All you need to do is to book a consultation with your local homeopath. In most of the countries, homeopathy is a very detailed study that takes at least four to five years. It is not something that can be learned in just a few months, so avoid 'homeopaths' with similar just a 'few-months-certifications'.

Finding a professional homeopath…?

From my own experience, the best homeopaths I have ever found and that helped me, were also medical doctors and so they could also combine two approaches and were not getting 'too carried away by the holistic world'. However, it's not the rule. I am just trying to underline the importance of confiding in only a highly qualified and experienced practitioner. I do have some general notions of homeopathy as I did study it, but my knowledge is too basic and so I simply do some general wellness coaching and I don't run a homeopathy consultation as I recognize my limits in this field. Unfortunately, not everyone thinks the way I do, and even the holistic world is also filled with some individuals who care more about their own financial wellbeing rather than their clients' wellbeing.

This is why, very often, people get prescribed homeopathy medications that 'don't do anything' at all. Trust me, homeopathy works- it only comes down to finding an experienced homeopathy practitioner.

There are also certain precautions to keep in mind, for example if you are perfectly OK and get exposed to a homeopathy treatments that you didn't need, you may start experiencing the symptoms it is supposed to treat. Then, there are also many advanced homeopathy treatments that may interfere with other natural therapies (when I was using homeopathy to treat my eye condition, my homeopathic ophthalmologist told me to abstain from Bach Flower remedies and phyotherapy) and even certain foods and essential oils (they may inhibit the effect of homeopathy).

Trust me: homeopathy is not 'just an herbal, feel-good' fad!

Bach Flower Remedies

Bach Flower remedies are another way of reducing stress and re-balancing yourself naturally. This is a system of 38 Flower Remedies that was discovered more than 80 years ago in England by Dr. Edward Bach. These remedies help to take out any negative emotions by flooding the body with the positive energies gathered from flowers (yea, I know it sounds weird and hippie dippie but read on).

When used in combination, the remedies can help restore joy and happiness. The remedies are wholly intended for self-care at home. The solutions are diluted in water and only a few drops are taken at a time. Of course, you would need to ask an experienced practitioner to prepare the Bach Flower drops for you, so that you can conduct the treatment. They are not meant to cause a dramatic change or healing, but they help to unpeel the emotions slowly and one at a time. It is even safe for pregnant women and children (again, under the guidance of an experienced Bach Flower therapist). You can also use it for animals. Whenever I travel, I leave my cats at home. One of them, always gets so sad, that she does not want to eat anything. My friend, Ana, who is an experienced Bach Flower therapist, prepared a special remedy for my cat, Uacia. It worked and my cat did not seem to be so stressed out about me not being around for 2 weeks. The poor cat probably feared that I was going to abandon her.

Bach Flower Remedies could be dubbed 'the younger siblings of homeopathy'. While homeopathy is much more complex and can be used to treat all kinds of imbalances and illnesses, the Bach Flower Remedies are only limited to balancing problems of a more emotional kind. This therapy is supposed to help you discover a new, happier and more balanced version of yourself and to connect with your real self and even purify your energy field (many energy healers I know here in Spain, also utilize Bach Flower therapy).

In the long run, they also bring benefits on a physical level as they can prevent many diseases from happening by simply regulating the flow of negative emotional patterns that, as Dr. Bach believed, are to be blamed for most of the illnesses. To be honest, I agree with him 100%. How many times did you get ill after having a stressful argument with a friend, relative, partner or your boss? How did that argument affect your quality of life that particular day? What did you do to control your anger, emotions, stress and prevent anxiety? Did you use any natural therapy to help eliminate the negative cause and pattern for possible negative behaviors and conditions? Or you just succumbed to it, became a victim, as a result did not felt empowered to take good care of yourself and got down with a flu or other condition a couple of days after? I am sure that you have been there at least once. I have! To be honest I think that everyone has. Personally, I believe that the most powerful strategy you can learn is to employ "mind over matter" and gradually learn how to control emotions. However, this is not as easy as it seems and so I recognize that at the outset of your journey, you may need some gentle, natural remedies.

The Bach Flower remedies don't fight/kill the actual bacteria/viruses that can cause disease/sickness but they can help prevent stress/life from causing your immune system from weakening, thereby keeping your body in shape for fighting off what causes non-stress based diseases naturally.

Here are some of them that are the most recommended in stressful situations:

Mimulus

- Mimulus can be used when a person feels fear, one that could be named, such as fear of losing a job, insects, and others. If a fear is so strong that a person trembles, then another remedy called Rock Rose can be used. If the cause of anxiety is not known, then Aspen flower should be used.
- Mimulus can also help to overcome shyness and is recommended for those who stutter and feel insecure in social situations. If you know exactly why you feel stressed out- Mimulus may be your remedy flower.

Cherry Plum

- This is helpful when the mind is stressed or over-strained. When a person feels like he or she is going to explode due to the stress, it helps bring back a semblance of self-control and relaxation.
- If you feel like you are in emotional crisis and feel overwhelmed, Cherry Plum might be your remedy flower.

Aspen

- When a person is fearful but without a known stimulus, aspen can help. An example situation of a people feeling anxious for no obvious reason is when they feel like they think something bad is bound to happen but then nothing happens, and they cannot tell anybody what they are anxious about.
- If you wake up, yet you can't get up out of fear and you feel like you can't face your everyday tasks because you are too scared in general (not knowing why), aspen can bring peace to your mind.

Rock Rose

- This remedy helps when people experience fright or terror, as well as when they are unable to think or move clearly because they have experienced some kind of a horrible event or trauma.
- Great for those who are paralyzed with fear and/or suffer from panic attacks.

White Chestnut

- This remedy is helpful to those who cannot sleep due to a mind cluttered with many worries and thoughts. The anxiety reaches its peak when a person wants to go to sleep.
- If you feel very tired throughout the day, yet cannot fall asleep at night due to the massive amount of uncontrollable thoughts White Chestnut can help you stop the vicious circle.

Red Chestnut

- Red Chestnut is helpful when people worry too much about the loved ones and keep thinking that something bad may happen to them. The thoughts become so persistent that a state of excessive anxiety is experienced. Red Chestnut can address those particular worrying feelings (about others) and bring an emotional balance so that you can start taking care of yourself as well.

Bach Flower remedies will be another effective weapon to fight off stress and even chronic anxiety...there is no limit to Bach flower remedies that can be prepared and adjusted depending on a treatment. Everyone is different, everyone is trying to overcome different problems and patterns...natural remedies mentioned in this chapter offer hundreds of solutions- there is also <u>your solution</u>. All you need to do, is to visit your local floral therapist and give it a try...

From my own experience: I first tried Bach Flower Remedies when doing my Reiki I attunement. My Reiki master, Oscar, is an experienced floral therapist and so he prepared some 'mysterious' floral mixtures for me and others who were doing 'Reiki initiation' to help us make the whole process easier. I was a bit skeptical at first, I kept saying: 'I only believe in homeopathy!'. However, the mixture I was taking had really positive effect on my life and made me much calmer and mindful. At that time, I was preparing myself to do my final exams in massage therapy. Being a quite ambitious person by nature- imagine my emotions! The Bach Flower remedies simply corrected certain imbalances and helped me confront things the way they were, without getting too emotional. The funniest thing is that even though I am not taking any floral remedies now, the effect still seems to be on. And the exams went just great. When you feel calm you ARE calm and you always to things right. You don't get too carried away by certain 'negative ambitions'. This is why I do believe that Bach Flower remedies may be useful as a temporary natural treatment in stressful situations that are difficult to control: break-ups, moving houses, moving to a different country or city, loss of a loved one, negative emotions that may it impossible to live peacefully, or other life situations that involve certain transformation that is feared or too much looked forward to. Emotional wellness is the key to personal success.

Chapter 5 Yoga for Holistic Relaxation

Meditative movement, such as yoga and tai-chi, are known to be very effective in helping people be relieved of the stress that they feel. It is natural and once you start practicing and mastering certain postures and sequences, you can always take it with you no matter where you go. To be honest, I prefer it to herbs, homeopathy or any other natural remedies that you have to take, and when you run out of them, you feel like you have nothing to fall back on. This is why, many years ago, I have committed myself to a regular yoga practice.

There were certain moments in my life where I would just fall off track and neglect my practice, but in the end, my body and mind would ask me to get back to it. Now, my preferred form of practicing it, is to squeeze in a few short sessions during the day, even when I am working. Whenever eating at home, I like to do a mini session before my meal. I have also created my own yoga rituals before going to sleep, after I wake up, or when I need more energy or relaxation. This chapter, of course focuses on relaxation.

Now, I am not a yoga teacher or a guru. I just want to share with you what I practice daily. As I mentioned, my relationship with yoga was a bit on and off. With all those "on and offs" included, I can say that I have been practicing it for 10 years now. One of my 2014 goals was to commit myself to a regular yoga practice, not necessarily long sessions, but regular sessions. I notice a big positive difference, peace of mind and better digestion.

I hope that you feel motivated to start. If you are like me and you have had this *on-and off relationship* with yoga, I encourage you to choose long-term, if not forever commitment to it. This is one of the best decisions you can make. Don't make the same mistake I made. Commit to it. Think when you will be in five years from now. Think of a strong body and a focused mind. Yoga will help you get there.

Yoga is all about progress. I know that I am not perfect. I am not like one of those super yoga teachers, even though I am quite flexible (not as much as I would like to, but I know that yoga is not only about being physically flexible, one must also work on their mental and emotional flexibility, right?). Remember again, yoga is about making constant progress and developing real self-confidence as a result. It's not about falling in perfectly into each pose or sequence. It's about overcoming yourself. To me, yoga is a constant personal battle for improvement. Monitor your progress; it will give you sensation if calmness and real self-confidence. This is a real body and mind therapy. *Forget about perfection, go for progress.*

I want to show you that yoga has benefited me in many ways and it has also liberated me in a way that I finally got rid of excessive ambitions and perfectionism. This "move" helped me find more peace in all other areas of my life. It also helped me become more patient with my other goals. Life is like yoga. Take small baby steps, breathe, focus on your growth, listen to your body and practice compassion.

Create your own yoga rituals to rejuvenate holistically. If you are pregnant, have undergone surgery, have any injuries or suffer from any serious medical conditions, please make sure you contact an experienced yoga professional before getting started on your practice. Poses that involve using abdominal muscles are very often contraindicated in menstruation.

Yoga

Regular practice can help you feel more strengthened, especially when you have to face stressful events, without becoming restless. Yoga practice entails the use of the asanas, or the body postures; the pranayamas, or the breathing techniques; ancient yoga philosophy, and meditation. These help patients who have anxiety disorders to recover faster as they are more positive.

Yoga postures can actually do more than just help the body become more flexible or relaxed – they can also help the mind and body become happy and healthy. The asanas help let go of tension and any negativity in the body, mind and spirit.

The most challenging thing for me, was to learn to breathe consciously while doing my asanas. Remember, breathing is even more important that being flexible or doing asanas in a perfect way. In yoga, you breathe in and out through your nose.

Sukhasana (Easy Pose)

This is a great pose for beginners. Start your yoga session with Easy Pose. Focus on your body, direct your breath to where the tensions are. You may also stretch intuitively.

Matsyasana (The Fish Pose)

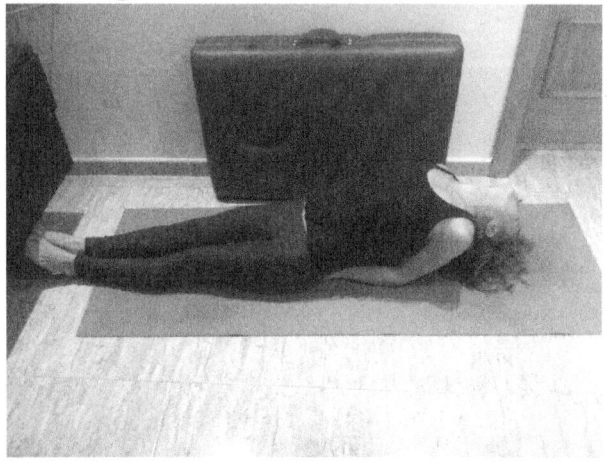

My yoga teacher has always instructed me to keep my eyes open when doing this pose. It helps work on your focus and inner strength. Plus- no more pain in the neck.

Setubandhasana (The Bridge Pose)

I love this pose. It is a form of self-massage for me. Helps me relax after long hours of physical and mental work.

Shirshasana (The Headstand)

Marjariasana (The Cat Stretch)

Then, you look up the ceiling so that your spine moves to the opposite pose ("U" shaped). Let's learn from cats! Breathe in (when you look up) and out (when you stretch back looking down again).

Adhomukha Shwanasana (The Downward-Facing Dog)

Paschimottanasana (Seated Forward Bend)

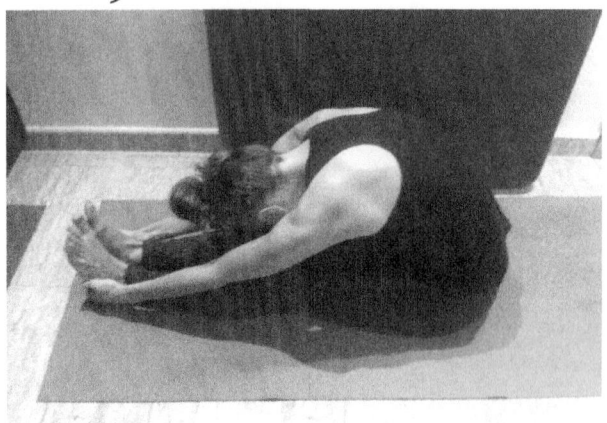

Yoga is not about perfection. It's about leaving all judgment behind and focusing on doing the best we can. Focus on the process and enjoy the journey.

-Balasana (Child's Pose)

Vrkshasana (Tree Pose)

This pose helps me gain strength and balance. I like to practice it in difficult and challenging moments. It is also very energizing. Again, breathe, breathe, breathe...

Halasana (Plough Pose)

I love this pose after long hours of computer work. It does wonders to my neck. This pose forms part of my evening yoga ritual as it relaxes me and helps me hit the sack.

After the posture session, lying down in the Savasana (Corpse Pose) can help the body and mind to have a thorough relaxation phase. Breathe slowly and relax like you deserve.

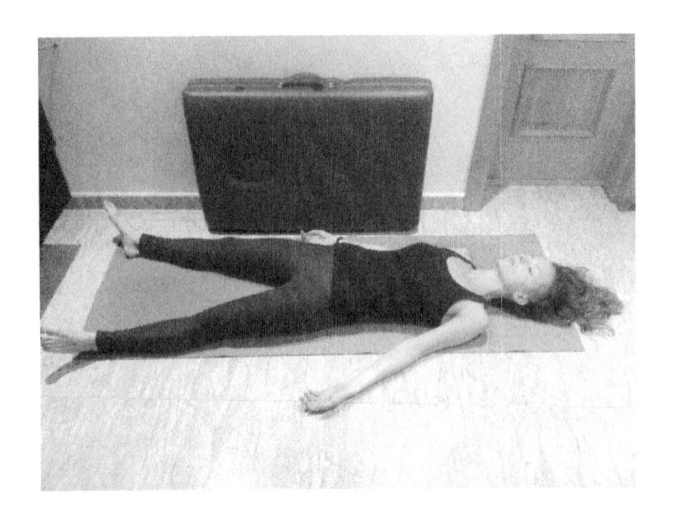

If you are not new to yoga, then make practice of those asanas your regular daily routine. It can also work for anxiety prevention. If you have never tried yoga, I suggest you join your local yoga classes. Most of the yogis are very positive and calm people and can have a great influence on you. Talk to your yoga teacher about your stress levels so that they can tailor yoga exercises especially for you and make them even more efficient. Finally, joining yoga classes will help you gain more positive outlook on life and meet some new people that can undoubtedly bring more happiness and peace of mind to your life that you can possibly imagine.

2. Breathe correctly with the help of pranayamas.

Like I said earlier, in yoga you breathe in and out through your nose. However when not practicing asanas, you can experiment with different breathing techniques. Choose what suits you.

Sit comfortably, close your eyes and place your hands on your knees. Make sure that you are sitting in a relaxed position so that you can relax your shoulders and become aware of all the tension accumulated in your body. Tell your subconscious: *I am going to*

breathe in all the positive energy that my body and mind need to start healing and I am going to breathe out all the unnecessary tension that is causing me pain and anxiety.
If your mind wanders, don't worry, accept it and take all the time you need to prepare yourself; don't force it, just let it come.

Now focus on your back. Make sure that you sit comfortably but with your back straight. Put one hand on your chest and the other on your stomach. Breathe in through your nose, the hand on your stomach should rise and the hand on your chest should move a little.

Exhale through your mouth, pushing out as much air as you can. Remember to contract you abdominal muscles and if you can, keep visualizing the black clouds leaving your body each time you exhale. While exhaling, the hand on your stomach should move in and the hand on your chest should move very little.
Continue to breathe in through your nose and out through your mouth. Try to inhale enough that your lower abdomen rises and falls.

This has been found to be effective in releasing any stress in the body. Exhalation is a lot longer than inhalation. Remember the basic rule: breathe often and deeply, inhale imagining the positive and vibrant energy filling in your whole body, and breathe out visualizing some dark clouds that are leaving your body so that peace of mind and profound relaxation can be achieved.
If you have never tried yoga before and are not sure how to go about it, here is my tip:
1. Find a class or a workshop locally (not on-line). This is important because you need a teacher who can actually give you some feedback and guidelines to stick to.
2. After you have grasped the basics, carry on your practice at home. Watch yoga videos and listen to guided meditations.

3. Read inspirational yoga books and learn new stuff.

Relax with Tai-Chi

Tai-Chi is an ancient tradition practiced by the Chinese that was originally used for self-defense. Nowadays, it has already evolved into an exercise that is graceful in nature, and it is used to reduce stress, as well as other health conditions. This is oftentimes described as a type of meditation in motion. Serenity is promoted through the use of gentle, flowing body movements.

There are numerous health benefits that the regular tai-chi practicing can bring:

-It promotes serenity and inner peace
-It balances flexibility and fitness
-It promotes body & mind control
-It creates the feeling of inner strength
-It gives the feeling of connectedness with the ´here and now´
-It prevents heart diseases
-It is used in eating disorders treatments
-It helps to fight depressive and difficult moments

It is all about taking action and fighting for your quality of life. It is also about eliminating bad habits that may only aggravate the problem and finding healthy solutions. Immerse yourself in the wonderful world of energy working like yoga and meditation. You will only need to make an effort once- just to get started.

I would recommend tai chi for those who want to experience a really deep energy working experience. It also work wonders for those who are recovering from injuries, as the movements are really slow and there is no stretching like in yoga.

As for meditation and yoga, it is always easier and more enjoyable to accompany them by music therapy, I recommend you check out YouTube as well as SoundCloud.com and search for relaxing sounds by typing in keyword(s) as: spa, yoga, meditation, relaxation, focus, Zen, Reiki and sleep music.

My personal thoughts on creating your own yoga...
To me yoga, is not only about doing the actual yoga poses. You may prefer to do other forms of physical activity, for example dancing, swimming, Pilates, and fitness. Yet, if you employ your mind, and commit to making a progress without making any judgment or beating yourself up, you will be making your very own form of yoga. Focus on your each movement when you exercise, try to work on your posture and breathing, you see, even when you go jogging or play basketball, you may be doing your very own kind of yoga. Do you agree with me? What is yoga to you? And what would be your very own, special style of yoga? Have you ever experienced this deep sense of connectedness, like "here and now" feeling when practicing sports?

Finally, yoga is not only about the actual yoga practice. You can take yoga philosophy I have just briefly discussed (be gentle with yourself, breathe, don't judge, practice compassion etc.) and utilize it with other sports, as for example swimming, fitness, weight lifting, running. Yoga has helped me gain more focus and vitality and so I was able to focus on other physical activities that involved more strenuous physical activity. What is fitness to me? It's not about overloading yourself with more than you can take, it's not about taking dozens of pills and supplements to keep you going.

Fitness is about feeling amazing and maintaining a balanced, vibrant health lifestyle.

Now, we all know that regular physical activity helps reduce stress; we all know that we can get rid of negativity when going on a long walk, running, spinning, cycling and doing other gym activities. We all know it, the problem is very often time.

Here is what I do- I make sure I can have at least 15 minutes daily to practice sports. 15 minutes is better than nothing, and it will give you the feeling of self-achievement and confidence. You will feel great in your body. Physical fitness is one of the best stress and anxiety killers. If it's not your habit yet, make it your habit now. Get started on your "15 minutes a day move your body" challenge. If you feel like you're falling off track, send me a message on Facebook or via my blog (HolisticWellnessProject.com). I will motivate you if necessary.

Become a "health investor". Invest time in your health. Don't invest it (or better said: "don't waste it") in social media, watching TV and indulging in anything that is not contributing to your overall wellness and health. Invest smart.

When I am really pressed for time, and I feel like I have too much to do and I begin to feel stressed out about it, I put my running shoes on, and I go for a quick run. I run up the hill, and the way back. The way back is easier of course and I always feel proud of myself that I managed to overcome procrastination (and whatever it was that my brain was telling me) and that I ran up the hill. I left all my worries and anxieties there, up on the hill.

Then, there is a relaxing shower and aromatherapy self-massage, something that we will be discussing at the end of this book.
To sum up: fitness is wellness and wellness is fitness. Commit yourself to exercising daily. Start with 5 minutes a day to create a

habit. Then, make it 10 minutes or 15 minutes. You will feel so good, that your body will naturally crave more physical activity. It's all about taking meaningful and purposeful action. You know your purpose. Now, focus on solutions. Most of them are within you and are free.

Chapter 6 Holistic Nutrition

"The food you eat can be either the safest and most powerful form of medicine or the slowest form of poison."

Ann Wigmore

Your diet also plays a vital role in helping you to not only feel free of stress and anxiety but also vibrant, healthy, with strong immune system. I am not here to tell you to follow any particular diet. Again, I just want to provide you with information and inspiration to create your own. I am a firm believer in the Alkaline Diet and a big fan of Doctor Young's books: *The pH Miracle*. I know that there are many skeptics who don't agree with him, but everyone that I know (including myself) who has ever tried this lifestyle, reported an increased feeling of not only physical but also emotional wellness- and this is what we are looking achieve through this book.

To make it very simple, the Alkaline Diet is not only about losing weight, it'd also about detoxifying and restoring your energy levels naturally. It's not just a diet. It is a holistic system and a truly holistic lifestyle. Even if you already have a diet that you want to stick with, you can always benefit by eliminating or reducing acid forming foods and adding more fresh alkaline foods to your diet. It's simple: eat a clean diet and add more fresh vegetables and some seasonal fruit.

If you have never heard of the alkaline diet before you can download my free eBook: "Revolutionize Your Life with Alkaline Foods". It also includes dozens of alkaline recipes as well as acid-alkaline charts that are reliable and accurate. They will help you grasp the basics. Your free eBook is waiting for you at: www.holisticwellnessproject.com/alkaline

Stress is acid forming and so cultivating a stress-free lifestyle and learning all about stress management, also forms part of the alkaline lifestyle.

Shelley Redford Young from PhMiracle.com says: " Physiology affects emotionality, and emotionality affects mentality". I totally resonate with this statement. Stress and anxiety are mental and emotional state, an imbalance that can be either reduced or stimulated by what we eat and drink.

"Take care of your body, it's the only place you have to live"- Jim Rohn

It's all interconnected. Even if you have mastered the art of relaxation but do not care about what you eat, you will be poisoning your body which equals to poisoning your mind and emotions as well. I guess that if you are reading this book, you agree with the holistic approach that I advocate. If not, do the experiment on yourself. Spend one month eating healthy and alkaline foods, walk regularly and do sports. You will feel amazing and you will most likely find success in other areas in your life. Now compare it to doing it the other way round- eat unhealthy, processed garbage and spend your free time watching TV instead of moving your body. How you will feel? Sick? Ill? Tired? This is the acidic state of mental fog that I want you to avoid. This state can only aggravate stress and anxiety. You need to focus on a clean diet, with wholesome foods, plenty of vegetables (especially green) and some fruits. Choose local organic products and observe how your body and mind will be grateful for this decision you are just about to make.

In this chapter I am going to suggest certain nutritional tips that I practice not only when I am stressed, but actually all the time. Healthy eating is my lifestyle. My nutritional patterns are of course influenced by the Alkaline Diet, the Macrobiotic Diet, the Vegan Diet (even though I am not 100% vegan yet) and the Raw Food Diet (especially in the summer, it's refreshing and provides plenty of nutrients).

Here's a quick, common-sense overview of alkaline vs acid-forming foods. What makes them "alkaline-forming" or "acid-forming" is the effect that they have on your body after they have been eaten, not before:

- Virtually all vegetables, especially green vegetables are super alkalizing. Try to add more salads, vegetable juices and smoothies to your meals.
- Everything that has been processed is highly acid-forming so eliminate processed foods from your diet and focus on natural, wholesome options.
- All forms of sugar are acid-forming and so are foods that have gluten/yeast
- Caffeine is acid forming. If you want to alkalize go for herbal infusions, clean alkaline water and vegetable juices
- Snack on healthy nuts and seeds. Add healthy oils like coconut oil and olive oil into your diet. They won't make you fat.
- Add more fresh fruits and vegetables into your diet. Non-sugary fruits (limes, lemons, grapefruits, tomatoes, avocados) are alkaline-forming (yes, lemons are acidic in their natural state but they alkaline-forming properties once metabolized) while other fruits are considered to be neutral. To get detailed charts, don't forget to grab the free eBook I recommended above

- Reduce animal products and focus on a plant-based diet instead. For example, quinoa meal will be much more nutritious and will provide you with more natural protein than meat. I am not saying you should go 100% vegan (unless you want to). I am trying to encourage you to explore some amazing vegan alkaline options. For example, coconut oil or almond milk is much healthier than cow's milk.

Here are a few of my general nutrition tips:

-Healthy grains
People who can tolerate gluten in their diet can get benefits from whole grain food, such as whole grain bread and rice. True whole grains are rich in magnesium, and it has been found that a deficiency with the said mineral can lead to anxiety. Whole grains also contain tryptophan, which then turns into serotonin, which is a neurotransmitter that helps a person calm down. I especially recommend quinoa that is actually gluten-free. You can also get gluten free oats, millet, amaranth, and buckwheat.

To learn more about quinoa and get some amazing recipes, check out my article:

www.holisticwellnessproject.com/blog/health-wellness/health-benefits-of-quinoa/

-Antioxidants
Foods rich in antioxidants help to fight off stress. Believe it or not- nutrition is also a natural healing therapy! As suggested earlier, try to turn to green vegetables and alkaline fruits such as lemons, limes, grapefruits and tomatoes.

Other great choices (not alkaline, but healthy) are blueberries, oranges, apples, acai berries, and bananas (again, we need magnesium and potassium). Add plenty of fresh organic green vegetables (spinach, kale, parsley) and use them for smoothies (almond milk and coconut milk are great for alkaline smoothies).

-Seaweed
Seaweed is said to share the same benefits as the ones given by whole grains. It is very nutritious, as well as contains a high amount of magnesium. To those who are gluten-sensitive, seaweed is a better alternative for whole grains. I recommend you start discovering algae such as wakame, kombu and hiziki.

-Almonds
Almonds are rich in zinc, which is a major nutrient needed to maintain a balanced mood. A zinc rich diet is recommended for those who suffer from constant stress or adrenal exhaustion. Almonds also contain healthy fats and iron and are really alkalizing. I also suggest you start using almond milk, almond butter, and almond powder that you can add to your smoothies for a strong start of a day. Almonds are great as a snack and you can also use them in salads and soups. Remember to use fresh, raw, organic almonds in their unprocessed form (anything else is acidic).You can also use crashed almonds (almond powder), add them to your meals, salads, soups and sandwiches. Almond powder is used as cheese replacement by vegans. Of course, I am not telling you to go vegan if you don't want to, but in my opinion it's always good to look for vegan alternatives as much as possible.

-Cocoa
Ok, it's time for a healthy treat...

Pure dark chocolate that does not have added milk or sugar is good for people who are stressed out or are anxious. It helps reduce cortisol, which is the stress hormone that triggers the onset of anxiety symptoms. Choose organic chocolate or cacao. Blend it with a banana, almond milk, a bit of spinach and add some spiruline or chlorella powder for more nutrition. Alfalfa green powder (extremely alkaline and full of minerals) is great too and it will make sure that your body has enough nutrients. This is a healthy alternative to unhealthy chocolate shakes and drinks that are full of artificial sugar and can make you feel over-stimulated and jittery.

Holistic Nutrition is about looking for healthy alternatives and solutions. It's not about going hungry or feeling deprived. It's about learning how to use food to balance your body, mind and emotions.

Here is a list of the foods **to avoid** when desiring to achieve holistic relaxation lifestyle:

-Foods and drinks that contain caffeine (this is a rule number 1!)

Caffeine is considered a notorious substance as it has the ability to trigger anxiety and panic attacks. It also increases the production of a certain chemical in the brain, norepinephrine, which makes a person awake and alert. Foods that contain caffeine can make a person more nervous, jittery, and excitable. From my own experience, ever since I reduced coffee and switched to an occasional cup of herbal tea or green tea, I became much calmer, more energetic and slept much better.

-Salty food

It is important to use salt in moderation in order to keep a healthy blood pressure. Excessive amounts of salt in the body can increase one's risk of developing heart problems, which then increases the stress in the body. When the body is in constant amount of stress, there is a higher chance of developing an anxiety disorder. I suggest you start using Himalaya salt as it is alkaline and full of minerals such as Magnesium, Potassium, Phosphorus, and Iron.

-Alcohol and Drugs

Even though alcohol has been seen to induce relaxing effects on the body, it has the ability to produce symptoms that are anxiety-like once it is metabolized. Withdrawal symptoms can further aggravate anxiety.

It is also advisable to avoid:

- Fried food
- High-glycemic carbohydrates
- Foods that have a high content of unrefined sugar
- Processed food, processed meat, pre-packed food

An example of a healthy and balanced breakfast to feel full of energy and vitality yet not nervous is:

- Healthy grains, like for example quinoa, integral rice, millet, amaranth or other with coconut milk or /rice milk/ or almond milk + a few slices of banana+ a few dried fruits or nuts+ a few acai berries (or other fruit you like). You can add a piece of algae (e.g wakame) or use alfalfa powder supplement.

My yummy and healthy full power breakfast (or snack before hitting the gym)

ANOTHER, SIMILAR BREAKFAST IDEA...

- Ideally, you would skip coffee or black tea and have a cup of green tea or any other tea I recommended earlier. You can also make a delicious juice to make sure that you keep your vitamin C levels high: orange, carrots, grapefruit, lemons. Experiment with your favorite fruits! My recommendation is to get Vitamin C naturally from Vitamin C rich foods. I am not a big fan of Vitamin C supplements as they can interfere with your liver and kidneys.
- Make sure you always carry a banana on you as well as other magnesium rich snacks
- Fresh organic fruits and vegetables as well as sprouts and nuts are your friends. Experiment with all kinds of juices and salads.
- Use organic cold-pressed oils, coconut oil, olive oil and avocado oil are excellent choices.
- If you eat meat, opt for organic as much as you can. That way you can avoid the massive amounts of toxins and antibiotics. Fresh fish, seafood and free range chicken are animal protein that I would recommend for those who are not vegetarian.

- Finally, make sure you eat enough. Food is life. Choose right foods that nourish your body and mind and you will live your life to the fullest.
- Practice mindful eating. Try to eat focusing only on your meal. Switch off the TV. Play some gentle music in the background. Make it your own ritual.

Further recommendations:

When it comes to nutrition as an anti-anxiety tool, the best thing you can do is to eat natural foods. By saying 'natural', I mean foods that were not manipulated nor genetically modified. It has been proven that our grandparents did not suffer from anxiety like we do now. The answer is simple: they ate healthy foods as everything was relatively healthy at that time.

Final thoughts on healthy eating

I believe that changing your nutritional habits into new, healthy ones is an amazing journey where you can discover the importance of self-care and how important it actually is to provide your body with the right tools so that it can heal itself naturally. Many people, when hearing the word "diet", only think about weight loss diets and getting "shredded". My first goal is a healthy body and a focused mind. I know that this is a must for me to feel healthy, motivated and energetic. I also know that my body deserves the best, this is why I really enjoy investing my time in healthy shopping, healthy cooking and learning new recipes as well. Did you notice that I used the word: "invest", instead of for example "waste?".

No matter which relaxation methods from this book you have decided to follow, your long-term goal and mission number 1 should be improving your nutrition and moving towards non-processed organic foods.

Like I said, I found my emotional wellness in Alkalinity. If it sparked your interest I suggest you check out the resources I mentioned in this chapter. If you are pressed for time and are not interested in reading long books or purchasing them, I suggest you visit my blog HolisticWellnessProject.com. The Alkaline Diet and holistic nutrition is one of my main focus there, alongside with general Wellness Coaching and Motivation for a Healthy Lifestyle. Big changes in your life may start from there.

Additional benefits that you will reap off will be more energy levels. This is why you will feel naturally motivated to hit the gym or do any other physical activity that will help you rid of stress. Not to mention a healthy and sexy body that you will feel proud of and that will inspire other people towards healthy eating as well.

Chapter 7 Mind over Matter

A lot of people who suffer from chronic stress and severe anxiety disorders actually go to support groups. The biggest benefit of attending support group therapy is that you will be able to see that you are not alone in the struggle – there are many other people who may experience the same problem, or even bigger problems. This revelation could give you a great relief. Truth be told, is that we are all in the same boat. Everyone experiences stress, but some people simply do not manifest it or suppress it. They may seem calm but deep inside they are shattered. This is just my personal observation.

Support groups can help if you are ailing to develop better or new skills when relating with others. It is important to learn how to interact with those who are in the group as the group mirrors the society. Once you know how to interact with the others in your group, you can also build stronger relationships outside the support group. The members who deal with a similar problem can then continue to support each other, and even come up with new and better ways of dealing with their problems. Sharing one's weak points, fears, negativity and other unpleasant emotions becomes something normal. It's good to get it off of your chest.

It may be a bit difficult for some to open up especially in front of strangers, but due to the fact that many share the same problems, it could be easier to discuss one's feelings. Remember that everything is also kept confidential.

You may be one of those people who prefer to confide in a relative or friend. Some people though, find it easier to open up to complete strangers and it is also a good idea to confide in someone that doesn't know you and can objectively view your problems without putting in any judgment or personal attachments. They can give you their honest feedback. Sometimes we experienced anxiety as a result of indulging in certain negative patterns or emotions, whether we realize it or not. Talking to a professional therapist may help expose those patterns and change them. The first consultation may be a bit painful: it is not always very pleasant to learn about what we do wrong. However, I recommend you simply change your way of thinking to: "in order for me to feel better I need to expose my negative patterns and learn about what can be improved about me, my lifestyle and my emotions".

In case of chronic and persistent anxiety disorders a regular therapy that is based on a mutual trust will bring many positive long-term results. The most difficult part is to choose the right therapist and to open oneself to a treatment. Don't be afraid to experiment and to change a therapist: as long as the reason for that is a desire to find the right specialist, it's something that I really recommend. However, don't force yourself into a therapy with a person you feel like you cannot trust. Follow your intuition and confide in someone that you know you can trust. Also be prepared- sometimes they may tell you things that you don't really want to hear...This is what happened to me once, and I felt like crying, yet I confided in my therapist and I did the right thing- I just followed her coaching. I realized that many of my negative beliefs were my own creation and learned how to eradicate them and how to be stronger...Trust me- one powerful session can change many negative patterns that you have created for yourself that unfortunately only added to your overall stress and even anxiety. Also, very often to fly high, one needs to fall...so don't worry if you need to touch the ground first in order to start flying.

Another alternative that you may want to contemplate is to join a happy, positive yoga group (just like I suggested in the previous chapter, most likely you will bump into positive yogis that will have a nice energizing effect on you) or any other workshops or courses there are. As long as you surround yourself with positive people, you will keep stress and anxiety away. This rule also works other way around- avoid negative people at all cost. Remember when in one of the first chapters of this book, I mentioned using technology and smart phones, and that there is a clear difference between people wanting to steal your time and your need to help other people? Well, the similar rule applies here. Unfortunately we don't live in a perfect world where one human being wants to help another at all costs.

There are also certain bitter individuals who only want to put you down and take your emotional wellness away. Those people are not worth even a second of your time. You may feel like helping them, that's fine. But if they don't want your help, let them remain where they are, and simply hope for the best for them. You are now creating a new, stress-free you. You are also changing your perception of certain situations and people. Your goal is to remain unperturbed, even if someone does not respect your time and peace of mind and does not care about your feelings.

There is plenty of new friends waiting for you and they will help you create your new, stress free lifestyle. You may be interested in checking out websites like for example MeetUp.com.

Make a list of your hobbies and activities that you really like doing. I am sure that you can also find many free workshops in your area. Even if you feel a bit anxious when it comes to meeting new people, remember: it's about overcoming your fears, not about escaping from them.

It has been scientifically proven that any kind of artistic, as well as physical, activity that one is also keen on doing is a *natural anxiety and stress eraser*. If you are at home now, reading this book- take a break and go for a walk. Breathe in deeply- you are erasing anxiety and creating a new, anxiety-free you!

Nature is a natural therapy and it's free. It's up to you, your free time and/or how you manage the time that you have to actually go and "indulge" in the healing powers of nature. This is my meditation spot, it's about a 5 minute walk from my house, do you have yours?

And finally...(I almost forgot)- I have two wonderful cats who help me feel incredibly relaxed and I learn a lot from them (they always know when to slow down and do yoga and tai- chi!)

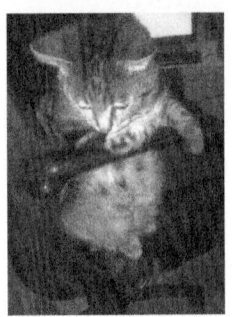

Chapter 8: Aromatherapy and Massage

We are finally approaching favorite therapies- aromatherapy and massage.

The therapeutic effects of massage have been known for centuries. Not only does it alleviate the physical pain but it also has a very positive effect on the nervous system. Although it is not the ultimate cure for anxiety it has proven to be a very efficient complementary therapy that makes an anxiety victim relaxed almost immediately and helps to achieve a peace of mind. As a massage therapist, I have noticed that manual therapy, when properly adapted, can bring an immediate body, mind, and soul relief for patients suffering from anxiety. It is also one of the most pleasurable natural therapies ever invented. As soon as the physical tension is eliminated, your mind and emotions feel a relieved too.

Healthy body= Healthy mind!

There are many kinds of massages that can be very helpful in fighting off anxiety and stress; I have listed some of them here:

Holistic Massage: not only does it work on the physical body and the physical pain but it also focuses on emotions and energy imbalances and blockages that add to anxiety as well as insomnia. Applying the oriental point of view, the therapist massages the body and also focuses on the energy centers and chakras that should be balanced in order to restore wellbeing and improve the energy flow. As a therapist I love combining Swedish massage with Reiki and guided relaxation to help my patients alleviate anxiety and stress.

Shiatsu: this massage works on the meridians, just as the Chinese acupressure and acupuncture does. There are no needles though and the shiatsu therapist will also use gentle stretching movements while working on certain acu-points to restore perfect balance. Regular shiatsu massage can also work miracles for chronic anxiety as well as digestive problems and eating disorders. I am not a shiatsu therapist, however I regularly use this therapy as a patient, and it is one of my favorites. It is much more than just a 'massage therapy'. It makes you feel really good in your body; focused yet relaxed, with high energy levels yet not over stimulated. A real holistic pleasure- always a winner.

Lymphatic Drainage: Although its main goal is to stimulate the lymphatic system, eliminate toxins, and stimulate the immune system, it also has a great relaxing effect on the central nervous system. The reason for that is that it employs gentle, repetitive and slow strokes that are sure to make you fall asleep. The sensation that you may get is like having a little cat walking all over your body, employing soft, intuitive movements. Facial lymphatic drainage helps prevent colds, improves skin condition, and alleviates headaches and eye strain. I really recommend it for those who suffer from insomnia and can't disconnect from their thoughts and everyday problems.

Face and Head Massage: all facial and cranial massages have been proven very effective in alleviating insomnia, anxiety and depression. You can choose Ayurvedic facials or Indian Ayurvedic Head Massage as well as European standard Swedish relaxing massage; or even facial and cranial lymphatic drainage that is also helpful in alleviating insomnia. Most people, when booking a massage, normally ask for a 'standard back massage'. However, when you think about it, when you feel really anxious, wouldn't you like to get a face or head massage? After all, the head centers the nervous system, which is why any face or head massage will help fight off anxiety.

Ayurvedic Massages: Ayurveda is not only about massages; in fact it is a science of life. Ayurvedic medicine recognizes the powerful and healing properties of massage that can be adapted and tailored for each patient, depending on a problem to be treated. In general, Ayurvedic massage for anxiety would try to reduce pitta qualities (everything related to stress, anger, hypertension, overreacting to problems) and stimulate kapha qualities (qualities related more to relaxation, peace and being calm). Ideally, an Ayurvedic doctor or massage therapist will design a series of massages for you combining it with Ayurvedic herbs and other natural remedies as well as a special diet to restore perfect balance and to fight off anxiety forever.

Neurosedative Massage: this massage is a mix of relaxing Swedish massage, breathing techniques, aromatherapy and kinesiology. Its aim is to relax the nervous system and eliminate the emotional pain so that the perfect harmony can be achieved. Personally, it is one of my favorite massage therapies as it really involves creativity. I truly recommend it, both as a patient and as a massage therapist.

Massage can be also combined with aromatherapy oils. Inhaling aromatherapy oils, or using them for massage, diluted with some good quality base oil, like, for example, coconut oil (you can also use them for self- massage e.g. after a relaxing aromatherapy bath) will bring an immediate relief and enhance your mood. The next chapter will provide you with specific guidelines.

Remember that essential oils are really multi-functional, for example bergamot can be used to calm down, relax, ease insomnia, stress and anxiety as well as fight oily skin conditions and dandruff (just to name a few). One essential oil opens a gate to a myriad of natural body & mind treatments.

These are some of the essential oils that I recommend for anti-stress treatments. I have also added their general properties, in case you want to learn more about them:
-ambrette (aphrodisiac, nervine, stimulant, stomachic)
-French basil (antidepressant, antiseptic, antispasmodic, cephalic, digestive, stimulant of adrenal cortex)
-bergamot (antiseptic, antidepressant, diuretic, deodorant, stimulant, stomachic, tonic)
-cananga (antidepressant, aphrodisiac, nervine, tonic)
-frankincense (anti-inflammatory, digestive, diuretic, sedative)
-hyssop (antiviral, cephalic, nervine, sedative, hypertensive, digestive)
-jasmine (antidepressant, antiseptic, aphrodisiac, cicatrisant, sedative)
-juniper (antiseptic, antitoxic, depurative, diuretic, nervine, sedative, aphrodisiac, stomachic)
-true lavender (antidepressant, antitoxic, diuretic, antiseptic, nervine, deodorant)
-lemon verbena (antiseptic, antispasmodic, digestive, nervous sedative)
-ylang-ylang (aphrodisiac, antidepressant, euphoric, nervous sedative, circulatory stimulant)

Bonus Chapter: Learn Holistic Facial Massage

It's time for you to get some new skills! This chapter is extremely practical and will teach you how to do the basic aromatherapy holistic facial massage to fight off stress and prevent anxiety.

First of all, you need to know the basics about the oils:

In case of a facial holistic massage, using oils is optional. You can also use an organic face cream. However, I recommend using oils as it will give you a chance to treat yourself with aromatherapy as well.

Choose an organic, cold-pressed oil of your preference. For example, it can be sweet almond oil, argan oil, coconut oil, avocado oil, or hazelnut oil (make sure that you are not allergic to them before you start using them).

For a facial massage, I suggest using one tablespoon of a vegetable oil and spice it up with only 1- 2 drops of an essential oil.

I always advise my clients to use their intuition. We only need the guidelines to get started- then we actually create our own style and our own treatments. Very often, we get attracted to fragrances that can help us- believe it or not!

Aromatherapy precautions to keep in mind:

Aromatherapy is a very safe and easy therapy to use, but keep in mind that there are certain precautions:

- Remember to wash your hands after applying aromatherapy massage.

- Do not apply the essential oils in their pure form as they may cause an allergic reaction. Instead, use blends that contain 2-5% essential oils diluted in good-quality cold-pressed oil.

- Do not apply oils after surgery (unless you have consulted with a doctor) or on open wounds, burns or rashes of unknown origin;

- Do not use the oils after chemotherapy (unless suggested by a doctor).

- Keep the oils away from the eyes and mucus membranes.

- Use the oils only topically (unless you have consulted with an aromatherapist who specializes in phytoaromatherapy).

- Avoid rosemary, thyme, Spanish and common sage, fennel and hyssop if you suffer from high blood pressure.

- Do not apply the treatments described in this book on babies or infants. It doesn't mean that aromatherapy can never be used on babies and infants, but extremely low concentrations should be used. Always consult with a medical or naturopathy doctor first.

- Make sure that you research the brand, read safety instructions for each individual oil you buy/use and check the expiration date,

- Store your blends in dark glass bottles, preferably in a cool, dry and dark place and remember to use within a maximum of one month after mixing.

Aromatherapy Blends/rules

The basic rules to keep in mind are the following proportions:

-For 15ml of vegetable oil (tablespoon) add 5- 7 drops of essential oil.

-For 2ml of vegetable oil add 1 drop of essential oil.

These rules usually apply to body massage, not facials. You may want to use less essential oils if you have sensitive skin.

My recommendation: If you are working on the face, use weaker concentrations, especially if you have sensitive skin:

For 15-30ml of a vegetable oil (or cream) use 1- 2 drops of essential oil. This is what I recommend for beginners. You can gradually make your blend a bit stronger.

If you wish to perform a facial treatment with aromatherapy oil, first apply the blend to the wrists to ensure that there is no allergic reaction. Avoid using oils like clove, cinnamon, oregano, rosemary and thyme if you have a sensitive skin that goes red easily.

Holistic Facial Massage Tutorial

Simple steps to perform a holistic facial massage

1. Mix the oils and apply small amounts at a time. Gently stroke the face with the pads of your fingertips. Do it slowly but try to maintain a steady rhythm. This gentle stroke is called neurosedative touch and it stimulates relaxation. Breathe in deeply, hold it for a few seconds, and then breathe out slowly.

2. If needed, apply some more oils to make sure that the skin is moist enough to do a massage, but avoid over-applying oils as your hands would then be losing contact with the skin. If the area gets too slippery, it's harder to do the treatment.

3. Using the area of the hand just below the thumb (the mound at the base) try moving your hand in circles around on the forehead. This technique will eliminate accumulated tension. Work on the forehead and then move to the temples, cheeks and chin area. The jaws can also accumulate great amounts of tension. If you feel any knots or tension, work the affected area a bit longer. Follow your intuition also as it tends to be much more effective than following massage protocols (which are good for getting started). Repeat a few times, doing one side at a time: work on the left, then the right side of the face. Keep switching. You may notice that one side of the face has more accumulated tension than the other. This is normal.

4. Using your fingers of both hands, gently make circles on the skin around the forehead, then move to the temples area and down to the jaw and chin area.

5. Using the pads of your fingers, gently squeeze the eyebrows and keep increasing the pressure. This technique is best performed employing your middle fingers and the thumbs. It also brings a great relief to the frontalis muscle and prevents migraines and headaches.

6. Using all your fingers - the pads of your thumbs plus the pads of the rest of the fingers - gently squeeze the chin and then move up to the jaws area. You may also want to experiment with moving your jaw to release tension.

7. Pressure points - For this technique, you will be using the pads of your thumbs (or middle/index fingers, whichever works best for

you) pressing different points on your face to enhance the therapeutic and healing effect of the massage.

Ayurvedic Massage and Shiatsu and Chinese Acupressure are all disciplines that work with these powerful points to stimulate healing. I only present an extremely simplified review of some of the oriental manual therapies, but you will be amazed at the results!.

Each point should be worked on for about 10-15 seconds and then released, and the whole procedure can be repeated again on the same point. Focus on the points that bring an immediate relief to you or your recipient as well as points that accumulate pain or tension. (This is a sign of some inner imbalance that can be healed with manual therapy.)

- Apply gentle but firm pressure to the middle of the forehead between the eyebrows. This point is called the Third Eye in Ayurvedic Medicine. *Then* work the eyebrows, simply applying the pressure on the points following the eyebrows line and stopping on the point where the eyebrows finish. Press it using the same technique and then work the temple areas. Applying pressure there can bring relief if you suffer from sinusitis.

- From the temples, start moving up following the hairline. According to Chinese acupressure, working on the hairline is an inseparable part of a face or head massage as it brings focus, concentration and calms nerves at the same time.

When your two hands meet in the center of the hairline, you can also apply the pressure to your scalp following the middle line. Get back to the hairline using the same path and move down to the *third eye* again and apply pressure.

- After working the *third eye*, apply pressure under the eyes in line with the pupils and hold for 10- 15 seconds. From there, move your hands down and work the corners of the mouth. There are pressure points approximately 1 inch away from the corners of the mouth.

- Gently rub the earlobes.

Going through the steps described above will bring feelings of relaxation and focus. Moreover, you can always skip the oils part and simply do the pressure points part, which is a great solution if you are at work or have limited time.

If you do it on someone else, they will almost certainly ask you to do it again.

Conclusion

Thank you again for taking an interest in my work. It really means a lot to me.

I hope it was able to help you realize that there are many paths that you can choose to successfully change your lifestyle into a balanced, holistic and stress-free (as much as possible) one.

Of course, I don't claim that reading this book alone will bring immediate results but I intend you to do everything you possibly can to successfully restore the body and mind balance the way you deserve.

The next step is to say *no to* stress and try to fight it with natural therapies. It is time for you to discover the new, relaxed you and choose the way you feel. My objective is to make you realize that there is the whole range of natural therapies that can help you achieve the peace of mind and the perfect balance so that you can be anxiety-free and enjoy all the amazing and beautiful things that the life can offer you.

It may be hard to begin with, it may be even harder to regain control over your emotions again, but it is definitely worth trying. Nature offers so many effective solutions that you are bound to be SUCCESSFUL and relax the way you deserve.

Finally, I need your help. Could you please take the time to share your thoughts and post a review! It would be greatly appreciated. I love hearing from my readers.

You can also contact me privately. If there is anything in this book that you did not understand or you did not like, or if you have any

questions or doubts, please send me an e-mail at info@holisticwellnessproject.com
I will be very happy to hear your feedback and to assist you.

For more inspiration and empowerment visit my blog:

www.HolisticWellnessProject.com

GET YOUR FREE GIFTS NOW

Remember to download your free guided meditations (audio) + free audio book (Mindfulness for Busy People) + free complimentary eBook (Holistically Productive) at:

www.holisticwellnessproject.com/minfulness

Enjoy!

With love, light, and WELLNESS,

I wish you holistic success in everything that you do,

Marta

MORE HOLISTIC WELLNESS BOOKS BY MARTA

To check out more of my books and articles (wellness, health, personal development, spirituality, spa, natural therapy, healthy recipes, alkaline diet, raw foods and much much more), please visit:

www.holisticwellnessproject.com/books

www.holisticwellnessproject.com/audiobooks

Finally, I would love to keep in touch with you for years to come!

www.facebook.com/HolisticWellnessProject

www.pinterest.com/MartaWellness

www.twitter.com/Marta_Wellness

www.linkedin.com/in/MartaTuchowska

Printed in Great Britain
by Amazon